Building a house that stands against the ravages of elements and time takes a skillful architect, a master craftsman, and tools of the trade deployed with wisdom and skill. There is no one I'd rather trust to guide me in the building of my soul's house than Dr. J.K. Jones, Jr., and in this wise and highly-readable book he offers readers everything we need to ensure our house is set upon a firm foundation. It's a primer on spiritual formation and much, much more. It's a blueprint for what God - the Master House Builder - is like, how we work alongside him, and how we overcome the hurry sickness that plagues so many of us. A book to savor!"

JEFF CROSBY
Author of *The Language of the Soul*

A Soul's House is the perfect guide for Pastors to give to their church as a way to develop their soul. While many books can seem overwhelming, J.K. finds a way to explain the unexplainable.

RUSTY GEORGE
Lead Pastor at Real Life Church
Author of *After Amen*

Over 25 years ago, I sat in Seminary under J.K.'s teaching, where the pages in this book were lessons in the classroom. Twenty-five years of life and ministry later- I am thankful that JK didn't want us to just know more about Jesus, but know Jesus more. I pray this book does what J.K.'s teaching has always done for me–deepen your love for our friend Jesus.

KYLE IDLEMAN
Senior Pastor at Southeast Christian Church
Author of *Not a Fan.*

If I was looking for a spiritual director, the first door I would knock on would be J.K. Jones'. In this book, however, J.K. comes knocking on my door! Picturing the soul as a house, he walks through my interior rooms, showing me how to best welcome Jesus into my innermost parts. For 35 years, J.K. has been the most helpful voice I personally know on deepening "spiritual receptivity," and this book feels like another dozen wise conversations over warm drinks on how to be formed in the image of Christ. Pick up this book, invite J.K. into your own house, and you'll be glad you did!

MATT PROCTOR
President of Ozark Christian College

A Soul's House stands out among the myriad of recent books on spiritual formation by delving deep into the 'why' behind spiritual growth. Dr. J.K. Jones, who has been guiding college and seminary students for decades, leads readers to recognize the continual need for renovating their souls. Whether you are new to your walk with Christ or have been on the journey for years, *A Soul's House* helps you understand that spiritual formation goes beyond a mere checklist of activities to complete. Instead, it is a lifelong transformational journey, empowered by God's grace and pursued for His glory, as beautifully explained in this book.

DR. TERESA WELCH ROBERTS
Professor of Ministry and Christian Formation
Ozark Christian College

Some things just go together—e.g. love and marriage, horse and carriage, and J.K. Jones and spiritual formation. And what God has joined together let no one separate. This work by my dear friend, is a primer, but it is so much more. It is a storeroom out of which J.K. brings things new and old (Matthew 13:52) from the wealth of his reading on this subject. He works through the spiritual house of his soul in tandem with one of his heroines, Evelyn Underhill. Not forgetting that God is the initiator of spiritual formation he defines it as God "using various means, in cooperation with our response, changing us to look like Jesus, in order to serve others to the glory of God" (pg. 25). Few writers turn a phrase and engage motivating metaphors like J.K.. You will want to read this book rapidly because it's a real page turner. But resist that temptation. Practice the discipline of slowing and enjoy.

DR. MARK SCOTT
Lead Minister at Park Plaza Christian Church
Online and Graduate Studies Professor
at Ozark Christian College

A SOUL'S HOUSE

A SOUL'S HOUSE
Copyright © 2023 by JK Jones
College Press Publishing Company
www.collegepress.com

ISBN: 978-0-89900-100-5 (paperback)
ISBN: 978-0-89900-101-2 (hardback)
ISBN: 978-0-89900-102-9 (eBook)
ISBN: 978-0-89900-103-6 (hardback with jacket)

Unless otherwise indicated, scripture quotations are from the ESV® Bible (The Holy Bible, English Standard Version®), copyright 2001 by Crossway, a publishing ministry of Good News Publishers. Used by permission. All rights reserved. The ESV text may not be quoted in any publication made available to the public by a Creative Commons license. The ESV may not be translated in whole or in part into any other language.

Scripture quotations marked MSG are taken from *The Message*, copyright © 1993, 2002, 2018 by Eugene H. Peterson. Used by permission of NavPress. All rights reserved. Represented by Tyndale House Publishers.

A SOUL'S HOUSE

**A Primer for
Spiritual Formation**

DR. JK JONES, JR.

"The soul's house, that interior dwelling-place which we all possess, for the upkeep of which we are responsible—a place in which we can meet God, or from which in a sense we can exclude God—that is not too big an idea for us."[1]

---

1. Evelyn Underhill, *Concerning the Inner Life with The House of the Soul* (Eugene, OR: Wipf and Stock Publishers, 2004), 65.

DEDICATION

TO MY KING

Jesus! The very thought of Thee, with sweetness fills my breast.
But sweeter far thy face to see, and in thy presence rest.
No voice can sing, no heart can frame, nor can the memory find
A sweeter sound than Jesus' name, the Savior of man-kind.
O hope of every contrite heart, O joy of all the meek,
To those who ask, how kind thou art!
How good to those who seek!
But what to those who find?
Ah! This nor tongue nor pen can show,
The love of Jesus, what it is none but His loved ones know[2]

---

2. Bernard of Clairvaux, "Jesus the Very Thought of Thee," in *Inspiring Hymns* (Grand Rapids, MI: Zondervan, 1969), Hymn 33.

CONTENTS

INTRODUCTION – Some Questions for the Soul's House.................. 13
CHAPTER 1 – A Starting Place for Renovating the Soul's House: Part 1 17
CHAPTER 2 – A Starting Place for Renovating the Soul's House: Part 2 25
CHAPTER 3 – The Soul's Long Journey to Know What God is Like: Part 1 ... 33
CHAPTER 4 – The Soul's Long Journey to Know What God is Like: Part 2 ... 41
CHAPTER 5 – Formation's House Builder: Essential Foundational Work ... 55
CHAPTER 6 – Working Alongside the Master House Builder................ 65
CHAPTER 7 – The Reading Room in the Soul's House..................... 75
CHAPTER 8 – What if My Soul's House Has No Reading Room?........... 87
CHAPTER 9 – A Room for Eating, Digesting and Ruminating on the Word.... 95
CHAPTER 10 – The Soul's House and the Needed Security System......... 103
CHAPTER 11 – Hurry Sickness and Information Overload in the House 113
CHAPTER 12 – The Soul House's Quest 127
CHAPTER 13 – The Soul House's Horizon: Formation's Long View........ 137
CONCLUSION – The Soul's House and an Ongoing Prayer 147
Bibliography 151
Acknowledgements 157

INTRODUCTION

SOME QUESTIONS FOR THE SOUL'S HOUSE

"When St. Paul described our mysterious human nature as a 'Temple of the Holy Spirit'—a created dwelling-place or sanctuary of the uncreated and invisible Divine Life—he was stating in the strongest possible terms a view of our status, our relation to God."[3]

How the Jesus follower is formed into maturity has been on my heart for nearly five decades. It was Evelyn Underhill (1871-1941), that gifted British Christian writer of the early twentieth century, who first made me aware of the soul as a house in need of renovation and "the upkeep of which we are responsible." The past forty-seven years of my life have been devoted to taking a long and intentional look at what it means to be changed into Jesus' likeness, in order to serve others, to God's ultimate glory. I have wanted to express my thoughts about this ongoing formation, but have not previously done this in a structured manner. In some ways, this book represents a long and wonderful conversation with Evelyn. I believe, for whatever reason, this is the right time to share my imaginative transformational musings with her.

---

3. Underhill, *Concerning the Inner Life*, 65.

There are four questions that have been on my heart and that I would like to invite you to mull over during this season, as the Lord directs you. As part of this process, place these four formational questions somewhere that you will see them daily. Perhaps on your refrigerator or on the mirror where you prepare for the day. Be open and hospitable. If the soul is a house where we can meet God, allow these questions to enter that house. I would have loved to have asked Evelyn these questions, but she died before I was even born.

The first question is this: **How can I turn my knowledge *about* Christ into knowledge *of* Christ?** I often meet people who appear to be experts at Bible trivia, but have never experienced a transformed life. I acknowledge that there is value in knowing the twists and turns of Scripture, in memorizing people, places, dates, and verses and being able to call all of that up at a moment's notice. But I am referring to something much deeper. So, my question is really important: How can I turn my knowledge *about* Christ into intimate knowledge *of* Him? This is worthy of great attention and regular prayer. Knowing about Jesus is not the same as knowing Him personally and deeply.

A second formational reflection question is this: **What do I intend to do with this knowledge?** Think about James 1:22; "But be doers of the word and not hearers only, deceiving yourselves." What will I do with what Jesus reveals to me about Himself? He leads the way, wanting us to know Him more intimately and to apply what only He can reveal to our everyday life. What do I intend to do? The word obedience has fallen out of favor in some contexts because of its overuse, but it is still a good word. As a result of Jesus revealing Himself to us, and because of the Gospel, this question is essential and worthy of deep reflection.

My third question is fundamental to what it means to know Christ. **At this place in my journey, what do I think is involved in truly getting to know Jesus more deeply?** Think about Philippians 3 again; Paul's admonition, his self-confession, is clear: "That I may know Him and the power of His resurrection and the fellowship of His sufferings." At this moment in our pilgrimage, and in this season in our spiritual journey, what place do our various spiritual exercises or holy habits play in our plan to know Jesus better? At this mile marker in our apprenticeship with Jesus, what do we believe is involved in getting to know Him more deeply? What place does the acknowledgment of our own pain play in this ongoing pursuit of knowing Jesus?

J.I. Packer was absolutely correct when he wrote, "What matters supremely is not the fact that I know God but the fact that He knows me."[4] Ponder that statement carefully. I will return to it. For now, how do you respond to Packer's insight? He is not diminishing our efforts to know the Triune God, but he is elevating our King's sovereign knowledge of all that He has created, especially us.

My fourth question is vital to our ongoing spiritual formation. **If I could change one thing about my interior world, what would it be? Why would I want to change it?** I am assuming that in our quiet reflections, we have thought about this. What would I change about me? What do I want Jesus to change about me?

Consider the faithful seeking of the great devotional writers, those I affectionately refer to as the dead guys: the monastics. These are men and women who followed Jesus wholeheartedly. Those ancient Jesus followers spent an enormous amount of time reflecting on what they identified as the seven deadly sins: pride, greed, lust, envy, gluttony, wrath, and sloth. I understand what they were trying to convey when they identified "the seven," but I think they drew the lines too closely. All sin is deadly. They should simply have said; "We are most vulnerable to these seven sins." What will our response be? In recognizing sin at work in us, is there one we could

---

4. J. I. Packer, *Knowing God* (Downers Grove, IL: IVP, 1973), 37.

claim and then say, courageously, "I want to change that unholy practice." What is it? Own it.

These are my starting questions; the place where I begin to explain my long view of spiritual formation. Years ago, at the start of my pastoral work at the Lake Fork Christian Church, in tiny Lake Fork, Illinois, I practiced a holy habit of prayerfully walking the streets of my village each Saturday and stopping here and there to hear people's stories. I did not have a name for my Saturday morning practice then, but I have since come to call it "Godspace." Other writers and preachers use this as a word that describes a slowing down, a way of being attentive to God and what He is doing in the life of His people. Here, God is a three-mile-an-hour God. He is not in a hurry. It is His divine pace in transforming lives that has intrigued me for decades. I want to talk about that here. Evelyn Underhill was right. The soul is a house worthy of making suitable for God's presence. Join me in that pursuit.

CHAPTER 1

A STARTING PLACE FOR RENOVATING THE SOUL'S HOUSE: PART 1

"First, we are led to consider the position of the house…
Our soul's house forms part of the vast City of God."[5]

Where do we start the renovation of our soul's house? Evelyn started with the position of the house. I know that there is a school of thought about spiritual formation and Christian spirituality that would begin this subject differently than I have. Often in the world of spiritual formation in general, there are questions that are asked immediately, like "Who am I?" I would call this an identity question. Once that question is answered, scholars, teachers and all who care about formation and Christian spirituality launch into a wider subject. Some will start with a vision question like, "Where am I going?" which catapults us into a conversation about formation. Some scholars want to start with an evaluation question like, "How am I doing?" or "What am I doing?" My preferred starting question is this; "Who is this Triune God?" We need to grapple with His identify before we can accurately

---

5. Underhill, *Concerning the Inner Life*, 66.

discover our own and discern what we are truly after. I believe that the kind of God we know becomes the fundamental question.

I want to start with this, and I hope you agree with my approach. I encourage us to slow our reading at this point, and ponder our spiritual journeys as we consider these questions: What are our earliest memories, our earliest impressions, our earliest recollections of what God was like or is like? Can we remember when we first considered who He was and is? This is difficult for many of us. I was asking a friend of mine how old he was when his father passed away. He shared with me that he was adopted. I hadn't known that important fact about my friend. He does not know who his biological parents were, and his adoptive father died when he was seven. I asked, "Do you have any memories of your adoptive father's death?" "No," was his reply. His only memories are second-hand, given to him by his adoptive mother. I realize that what I am asking here about God could be like my friend's experience, and is complex for some of us. Think back to that God-awakening moment, even if you were very young. What were your earliest impressions of God?

My heart's intent is not for this to be painful or traumatic for any of us, but in order to continue on this path, we have to do some hard work. I like to read Christian scholars and writers whose voices come from outside the United States. One of those is Trevor Hudson, a South African Jesus follower and author. He is Methodist by heritage. Trevor says, "The way we live is profoundly shaped by our picture of God."[6] Hudson is absolutely correct.

Our pictures of God can be redrawn. Whether we acknowledge it or not or can name it or not, our picture of God becomes the primary lens of our worldview. Dallas Willard, though maligned by critics for some of his writings, was right about the essential importance of our view of God. Willard

---

6. Trevor Hudson, *Christ-Following: Ten Signposts to Spirituality* (Grand Rapids, MI: Fleming H. Revell, 1996), 22.

taught philosophy at the University of Southern California and has left a deep and lasting impact on the Christian landscape. Trevor Hudson makes this observation about Dr. Willard: "Dallas Willard has pointed out, we live at the mercy of our ideas, we would be wise to reflect carefully on those that we have about God."[7] That, my dear reader, is a powerful statement worthy of consideration.

I could share endlessly about the importance of having the right view of God, but every time I dwell on this, I run headlong into a succinct story that the great C.S. Lewis told in *Mere Christianity*. He described the right view of God better than I can. Lewis awoke one night with a toothache. Lewis said,

> "I was so afraid to get up and go tell my mother that I had a toothache because I knew what my mother would do. She would give me an aspirin to take the edge off, but then in the morning she would call the dentist and I would have to go to the dentist. I knew all about dentists. You give them an inch and they take a mile. They are not going to be happy with just looking at one tooth. They are going to want to look at my whole mouth."[8]

Lewis goes on to say, "God is like that. God in some way is like a dentist. He's not going to be happy just looking at one little aspect of your dental hygiene. He wants it all." Knowing that God cares about "every aspect," what factors might contribute to our wrong view of God?

I acknowledge the profound impact of Don Willett and his *Stages of Faith: 8 Milestones that Mark Your Journey* workbook as key in shaping my own thoughts and what I share in this section of the primer. I cannot recall every source, but I am truly grateful for Dr. Willett. Here are three factors that may contribute to an incorrect view of God. **First, some of us may**

---

7. Hudson, *Christ-Following*, 25.
8. C.S. Lewis, *Mere Christianity* (New York, NY: Macmillan Company, 1956), 157-158.

have experienced a series of negative interactions with key people in our life that prevent us from seeing God clearly. My own story falls heavily into this first possibility of what might contribute to a false view of God. I had a father who could never be pleased. He was abusive when he was present, even though he was absent much of the time. My mother was left to raise us. My father was an angry man, mostly due to his prisoner of war experience and his battle with post-traumatic stress disorder. Some of you may have experienced a mother who just did not have the capacity to express the kind of tenderness that your soul desperately needed. There may have been a teacher who contributed to your warped view of God. Maybe it was a significant teacher whom you trusted, who then embarrassed you publicly. You might have had a relative who abused you physically or emotionally.

Not long ago, my wife and I were having our morning coffee. An infomercial appeared on our television. We typically mute those, but this was about the Boy Scouts and a lawsuit that was pending for scouts who have been abused. My wife let out an audible gasp. Her father was a scout master and if he learned about these sexual abuse cases it would devastate him. He is now in his late 90's and does not always pay close attention to what is going on culturally. He would be brokenhearted to know that a scout master would violate a sacred trust and abuse a young person. My point here is a simple one. Our incorrect view of God can be due to a variety of heart-wrenching experiences. People who believe God is capable of any of these abuses could also believe that He is no better than a cold, lifeless statue.

Second, some of us may have mistaken a guilty conscience for the voice of God and because of that guilty conscience, we've created the wrong portrait of who He is. I have a beloved friend who has talked about this publicly and would not mind me sharing this. He admits that he was born with enough conscience for the whole world. If he does anything that hints of being wrong, even though Scripture might be silent on the subject, my friend is weighed down by guilt. His well-intentioned, but legalistic upbringing wounded him. He is always checking his conscience. My friend is not alone in this. Paul did it. He had been raised in the dogma of the Pharisees, so this is understandable. This is not a condemning judgment upon his transformed life, but note that in Acts 24:16 he wrote, "I exercise myself to always have a conscience that is void of offense." The commitment to be "void of offense" is a full-time job. I didn't get an overabundance of that, but still my own conscience plagues me at times. I am prone to all sorts of tricks and snares from the enemy, the devil. I have mistaken a guilty conscience for the voice of God. God knows our sin-fractured lives. He is not a demanding perfectionist, even though He alone is perfect. Some of us think of God as a drill instructor. If you served in the military, you may think of a drill instructor you could not please. People who know God like that; a God who pricks their conscience constantly, would picture God as a colossal eyeball—always watching. God, for some, is like Santa Claus, searching every home for those who are naughty or nice. A God like that is intrusive and invasive because of an overactive conscience.

Third, some of us may have experienced false or inadequate Bible teachings that have crafted in us a wrong view of God. For many of us, warped Bible teaching has been a major barrier to knowing the true nature and character of God. This wall between ourselves and God is the result of false teaching. The person who has been influenced by this issue typically grew up in an environment where the Christian life was viewed in terms of a legalistic code. There is a legitimate place for keeping commands, but that is not the avenue through which one comes to know God. There is a whole realm of Bible teaching that views grace with suspicion. I recall as a young pastor being told by one of the church members, "J.K., you are really at your best when you break my heart, when you make me cry. I don't feel like you are preaching unless you step on my toes." I said to him, "I think you need counseling. You don't need me to beat you up every Sunday. If that's what you think the Jesus-following life is, you are mistaken."

If God is full of expectations that cannot be met, then God is a divine killjoy who delights in squelching anything that is full of compassion, love and grace. If God is that kind of God, then He is like a traveling evangelist who does not live what He preaches. That God is someone who always seeks to get the upper hand on His listeners, while He proclaims hell, fire and brimstone. That kind of God cannot be pleased. God is like that for some people because of what they have been taught. The people I am describing have never seen Scripture as a cohesive story about the good news of what God has done, is doing and will do for us in Jesus Christ. They've never put the pieces together. They have never recognized that grace always precedes the law. A lot of people have never grasped the foundational truth of the gospel and because of that, their view of God is skewed, twisted and warped.

In these many years of ministry, every time I have an encounter with a Jehovah's Witness or a Seventh Day Adventist, I am reminded of a demanding God. The primary false teaching they offer is to minimize the supremacy and sufficiency of Jesus Christ. Whenever false teachers diminish the person of Jesus Christ, they create a vacuum filled with laws and rule-keeping. Grace is lost. Joy is forfeited. Dane Ortlund gives us the just-right illustration. He writes:

> "A compassionate doctor has traveled deep into the jungle to provide medical care to a primitive tribe afflicted with a contagious disease. He has had his medical equipment flown in. He has correctly diagnosed the problem, and the antibiotics are prepared and available. He is independently wealthy and has no need of any kind of financial compensation. But as he seeks to provide care, the afflicted refuse. They want to take care of themselves. They want to heal on their own terms. Finally, a few brave young men step forward to receive the care being freely provided. What does the

doctor feel? Joy. His joy increases to the degree that the sick come to him for help and healing. It's the whole reason he came. How much more if the diseased are not strangers but his own family? So with us, and so with Christ. He does not get flustered and frustrated when we come to him for fresh forgiveness, for renewed pardon, with distress and need and emptiness. That's the whole point. It's what he came to heal. He went down into the horror of death and plunged out through the other side in order to provide a limitless supply of mercy and grace to his people… Jesus doesn't want us to draw on his grace and mercy only because it vindicates his atoning work. He wants us to draw on his grace and mercy because it is who he is."[9]

The starting place for soul renovation, for being changed into the likeness of Jesus Christ, is having the position of the soul's house set with the right view of God.

---

9. Dane Ortlund, *Gentle and Lowly: The Heart of Christ for Sinners and Sufferers* (Wheaton, IL: Crossway, 2020), 36-37.

CHAPTER 2

A STARTING PLACE FOR RENOVATING THE SOUL'S HOUSE: PART 2

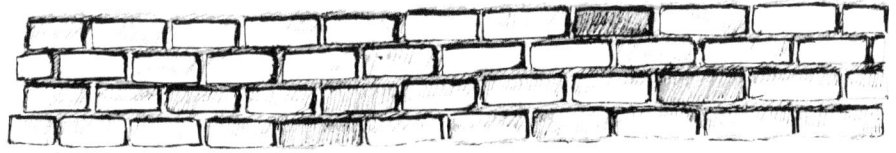

> *"But the soul's house will never be a real home, unless the ground floor is as cared for and as habitable as the beautiful rooms upstairs."*[10]

Evelyn was aware that our soul's house, if it were to be a real house habitable for our Triune God, required intentional care, especially the ground floor. The question that best helps with the renovation process is this one. What is God truly like? If we can get to the bottom of that question, we will find the lifelong joy of knowing Him as good, loving and faithful. From my humble vantage point, that is the essential question and the necessary starting place for spiritual formation. In the previous chapter, I listed three potential landmines that can skew our view of God. Now I want to suggest two more. **Fourth, some of us have experienced a traumatic circumstance or painful event for which we blame God.** This trauma can be the death of a beloved family member. Many of us have experienced this kind of loss and

---

10. Underhill, *Concerning the Inner Life*, 69.

grief. I am one of seven siblings. I recall the death of one of my brothers, the fifth child in our family. My brother died at birth. When he died, my mother went into a tailspin of depression. I have written about this elsewhere. My own words sting:

> "I have been thinking about a time when there was a seventh child in our family. Somewhere between my brother, Stephen, and my brother, Mark, my mother found out she was expecting another baby… Somewhere on that wondrously mysterious road between conception and birth, he died… I remember that my two older sisters and my younger brother knew that something was wrong. A baby-sitter came to the house to watch us. That seldom happened at our home. When Mom came home from the hospital, I remember looking into her face and seeing this lovely, sweet woman, crying the silent tears that only a woman who has lost the irreplaceable can understand. She went straight to the bedroom and I don't recall anyone speaking a word the rest of the day, except in whispers."[11]

For years, my mother kept her grief private. I threw caution to the wind and decided to send her the chapter I had written in the above-mentioned book. I was not sure if she would read it or even respond. Her pain was buried so deeply in her mother's heart. Mom did respond to my writing and my remembering the loss of my brother. To her dying day she thanked me for remembering, for trying to articulate her heartache. "Thank you," she said. "Thank you for remembering. Thank you for reminding me that I had twisted who God was. He had a greater good in all of this, that I could not recognize back then."

There are many people, who because of a loss of a significant person in their life, have a warped view of who God is. It doesn't even have to be the loss of a person. It could be the loss of income. It could be the loss of a

---
11. J.K. Jones, *Waiting on God: Trusting Him in Times of Suffering* (Joplin, MO: College Press, 1996), 86-87.

job. Think about people today in our COVID-ravaged culture. Counselors are overwhelmed with people who need to talk about their grief. Think of a dream that you've had, a hope that was crushed because of something that you had no control over. Consider a life plan that was blown apart. Consider the trauma of divorce. For someone who has experienced these kinds of heartaches, God may seem to be a God doling out punishment. He becomes the creator of crisis. If you want a clear example of this view of God, think of the Wizard of Oz. The man behind the curtain instilled fear and trepidation in Dorothy, the lion, the scarecrow and the tin man. For some, God resembles that mad Wizard of Oz, pulling levers, and caring nothing about those who are simply trying to get home—trying to find their way home to Kansas. Many people have experiences like that repeatedly. Job's wife struggled to make sense of her husband's loss of health and the death of her ten children. She encouraged Job to blame God. She said, "Curse God and die" (Job 2:9). This wrong picture of God warps our worldview and wrecks the house of the soul and its ongoing renovation.

Fifth and finally, some of us have experienced a false view of God due to our own personal misinterpretation or misapplication of Scripture. We read the Bible without employing proper interpretive principles. We ponder passages like Matthew 5:48: "Be perfect as your heavenly Father is perfect." We never look at what is called literary context. We never look at what is being said by Jesus in His famous Sermon on the Mount. We treat that passage and similar ones as biblical bludgeons. We believe that God demands a degree of perfection that we cannot deliver. God becomes our Egyptian emperor Pharaoh, decreeing not only that that we produce bricks, but that we find our own straw. Or God is Ebenezer Scrooge and we are Bob Cratchit in Charles Dickens' classic, *A Christmas Carol*.

At some point in your Jesus-following life, you must ask yourself; What kind of God do I know? What notions have influenced how I view God?

You must own that. I like asking questions of my interior world and my soul. Here are some questions that help me sort out the kind of God I truly know: Do I believe that God wants to know me and relate to me personally and intimately? Do I feel that God is for me or against me? If I believe that He is for me, upon what do I base that belief? If I believe that He is against me, upon what do I base that conviction? As I have taught my undergraduate university students: "You can actually study your way into wholeness. You can take this book, the Bible, and devote yourself to it. Read the four gospels. Read Matthew, Mark, Luke and John and study your way into wholeness. The Holy Spirit will be at work as you dig into these pictures of what God is like in Jesus Christ. You will find something that you have not found yet." I still share those words with people who struggle with their view of God. I even repeat them to myself.

When life goes wrong, and it will inevitably go wrong, do I assume God is punishing me? If I make that assumption, upon what do I base it? I got cranky a few months back with my small group. Somebody made a passing comment about how they believed that COVID-19 was the judgment of God. My right leg started bouncing up and down and I found myself wanting to say something. I wanted to enter into the conversation, to edit it and require a restatement, just as I would if I were the one who had misspoken. I don't know if I handled it well or not. I have learned that I articulate my thoughts better when I write them out rather than talk them out. Samuel Johnson, the great English scholar, said that writing makes a person exact. So, I wrote about what happened in my small group, about why I don't believe COVID-19 is the punitive judgment of God. I would not object to someone saying, "God is using this to purify the church. God is calling the church to be His righteous bride." If you want to label this pandemic as a purifying agent, I can honor your statement. However, to imply that COVID-19 is an expression of God's anger, that this pandemic is His wrath, misses the entire gospel story. All of God's judgment was heaped upon Christ at the cross. I cannot agree with a pronouncement that COVID is the judgment of God without some clarifying word. I clearly understand that people are trying to sort things out as we are constantly bombarded with crises in our cities, suggestions that we defund the police, infighting over gender identity, racial inequality and political hate speech. The truth is that all of us, and I include myself in this, are often sloppy with what we say and how we say it. Our constant complaining and conjecture ends up insinuating that we have a God who is bringing retribution on our culture. We are forgetting God's grace shown to us through Jesus Christ when we let our complaining and conjecture take over.

If I could draw a picture of God, what kind of picture would I create? I'm not an artist, although I wish I were. I recently discovered that one of our former presidents, President George W. Bush, has taken up painting. If I could paint, if I could draw, if I could sketch a portrait of God, what would He look like? I invite you to ponder that question with me. I want to give you a formational definition of our topic before I close this brief reflection. I've tried to shorten it without success so for better or worse, here is my definition of spiritual formation:

"God the Holy Spirit takes the initiative, through various means, in cooperation with our response, changes us to look like Jesus, in order to serve others to the glory of God."

Please slow down and notice the pieces of my definition. *God the Holy Spirit takes the initiative.* This desire to know God and be known by Him does not start with you, or with me. He is the one who initiates the relationship that we are pursuing. *Through various means* is a reminder that God the Spirit uses things like circumstances, heartache, sacred friendships, and holy habits to transform us. God the Spirit has a huge toolbox. There *is* a part that we play. It is why some of the great church fathers like John Chrysostom thought of the Christian life as a sacred dance between us and God, always remembering that God is the lead partner. *In cooperation with our response* is my way of saying that there is something that we lean into, someone we commit ourselves to and want to know. *Changes us to look like Jesus* is a simple way of saying that God the Spirit does the changing. We stay close to Him, because He is the change agent. Even Alexander Campbell, that conservative voice of the Church of Christ and the independent Christian Church, acknowledged that the Jesus-following life is best expressed this way. We are changed when we come within listening distance of God. He speaks change into our lives. We come within listening distance of His Word and that changes everything. None of this metamorphosis entitles us to say, "Look at me. Look how beautiful I am. See how great I have become." No, none of this makes us super Christians. All of this is ultimately about doing what Jesus did, as recorded in Philippians 2:6-11.

Christ emptied Himself by taking on the form of a servant. Some scholars say that paragraph was a worship hymn that believers sang. In that magnificent passage, I think Paul was saying that we "empty ourselves" as Jesus emptied Himself. We take on the form of a servant and serve others. We do this not for our own advancement, not for our own popularity, not for our own recognition, but for His glory. This is why I end my definition with this reminder; *in order to serve others to the glory of God.*

What is God like? We must start with that core question in this long formational journey. A.W. Tozer, the brilliant twentieth-century preacher and author, told us why we must think rightly about God. He wrote:

> "What comes into our minds when we think about God is the most important thing about us… What comes into your mind when you think about God?… The man who comes to a right belief about God is relieved of ten thousand temporal problems… The heaviest obligation lying upon the Christian Church today

is to purify and elevate her concept of God until it is once more worthy of Him—and of her."[12]

This is our starting place. Our soul's house must have the right view of God.

---

12. A.W. Tozer, *The Knowledge of the Holy* (San Francisco, CA: Harper & Row, 1978), 1-2, 4.

CHAPTER 3

THE SOUL'S LONG JOURNEY TO KNOW WHAT GOD IS LIKE: PART 1

> *"We are required to live in the whole of our house, learning to go freely and constantly up and down stairs, backwards and forwards, easily and willingly, from one kind of life to the other; weaving together the higher and lower powers of the soul, and using both for the glory of God."*[13]

"There is none greater than this God, not because he is merely a greater version of ourselves but because he is nothing like ourselves,"[14] said Matthew Barrett. Evelyn recognized this fundamental truth about God. To put it simply, she understood that there are two elemental sides of God. There is the side that seems beyond us and there is the side that we believe we recognize and understand. These two sides of God are seamless, but for the sake of clarity, I would like to explore them separately. The first side is the unknowable side of God. The theological term for this is "transcendent."

---

13. Underhill, *Concerning the Inner Life*, 74.
14. Matthew Barrett, *None Greater: The Undomesticated Attributes of God (Grand Rapids, MI: Baker, 2019)*, xvi.

By this term theologians mean the vastness of God, the God who is "other" than us, the God who is not like us. Sometimes this side of God is called the incommunicable side of God. This is the absolutely boundless, ultimate, not like me, far-from-me God. As we think about this God, we think about Isaiah 55. There, God tells us, "My thoughts are not your thoughts. Your ways are not my ways." Let me share four ways of thinking about the unknown side of God. In considering this side of God, I long for another way of taking the long journey to know this transcendent God, but inevitably I come back to four words that describe this aspect of Him. I share this as simply as I can.

#1. God is independent. That is part of what I mean by the unknowable side of God; the transcendent, incommunicable side of God. He is independent of us. A word that you will hear theologians use sometimes for this aspect of God is "aseity." This means that there is a self-existent side of our Triune God. This deep talk about God gives some of us a headache. We confess that we have never heard this word before, let alone considered it in thinking about God. This self-existent side of God makes it clear that He does not need you or me. He is above creation and yet He is the Creator. This is the omnipotence of God: all-powerful and uncreated. Exodus 3 demonstrates this aspect of God's attributes. Yet we are trying to talk about something that is beyond our comprehension. Consider the burning bush encounter between God and Moses as Moses was keeping his father-in-law's flock near Horeb, the mountain of God. The bush burned but was not consumed. He heard his name called, "Moses, Moses" (3:4) and heard God's pronouncement that he was standing on holy ground. Then God said: "I am the God of your father, the God of Abraham, the God of Isaac, and the God of Jacob" (3:6). Moses, terrified, hid his face. "I am" became so holy for the people of Israel that they would not pronounce it aloud, but referred to God as Adonai. Our best guess is that this word is pronounced "Yahweh" but we cannot know. The Great "I Am" instructed Moses to go to Pharaoh and bring the children of Israel out of the bondage of Egyptian slavery. A very overwhelmed and uncertain Moses raised the question, "But what if somebody asks me who You are?" And God repeated, "I Am who I Am. Say this to the people of Israel; 'I Am has sent me to you'" (3:14). That incredible and unheard-of description from God comes as close to explaining His independent nature as any other Bible passage does.

John 5:26 is also helpful in painting a picture of this independent side of God. Jesus, talking about God the Father said, "He has life in Himself." In other words, God is independent of us. There are many other sections of Scripture that give us glimpses into the transcendent nature of God. Many of the Psalms remind us of His independent powers. In Acts 17:24-25, the Apostle Paul was preaching at the Areopagus in Athens, Greece. In attempting to describe the nature of God, Paul said, "The God who made the world and everything in it, being Lord of heaven and earth, does not live in temples made by man, nor is he served by human hands, as though he needed anything, since he himself gives to all mankind life and breath and everything." Paul affirmed that God does not need anything from us. He was, is and forever shall be independent of us. God "works all things according to the counsel of his will" (Ephesians 1:11).

Again, I'll refer to "the dead guys," meaning the great devotional writers and theologians from the past. Often, they bring clarity to the transcendence of God. I remember these words from Clement of Rome (35-99 AD). Clement said, "The God of the universe has need of nothing." That one sentence helps me greatly and resonates in my soul. God is independent of you and me.

#2. God is indefinite. Without disrespect, I mean that God is the divine Energizer Bunny. He goes on and on and on and on. He does not stop. He does not sleep. He is without end. Another word that we use that sometimes helps us understand this attribute of God is the word infinite. Sometimes you will hear theologians, people like J.I. Packer, use this kind of language.

He writes:

> "How may we form a right idea of God's greatness? The Bible teaches us two steps that we must take. The first is to remove from our thoughts of God limits that would make Him small. The second is to compare Him with powers and forces which we regard as great. For an example of what the first step involves, look at Psalm 139, where the psalmist meditates on the infinite and unlimited nature of God's presence, and knowledge, and power, in relation to men. Man, he says, is always in God's presence; you can cut yourself off from your fellow-men, but you cannot get away from your Creator… And just as there are no bounds to His presence with me, so there are no limits to His knowledge of me."[15]

Packer and others like him speak eloquently of God's omniscience. He is omniscient in power and knowledge. That means that God has no limits in what He is able to do and what He is able to comprehend. He has no boundaries. The Scriptures remind us of this truth repeatedly. For example, Psalms 90:2 has that wonderful little refrain, "He is everlasting to everlasting." How are we to explain "everlasting?" Any attempt hits a wall in any language. Revelation 1:8 is the familiar line that John used to introduce us to his revelation of Jesus Christ. John said of Jesus: "He is the Alpha and Omega, the beginning and the end." There are other passages that underscore this characteristic of God. Consider Deuteronomy 33. It is one of those magnificent Old Testament texts about Moses. He was sending the tribes of Israel across the Jordan into the promised land. He realized that he would not go along due to his disobedience in striking the rock rather than speaking to it (Deuteronomy 32:48-52). Many years later, Paul identified that rock as Christ (1 Corinthians 10:4). Again, we are left to ponder and wonder. Moses said of God, He is "the eternal God" (Deuteronomy 33:27).

---

15. Packer, *Knowing God*, 75-76.

God is indefinite. Our creator goes on and on and on and on.

As a twenty-year old, I joined a group of airmen to attend a Navigator discipleship training week in Ocean City, Maryland. At the end of the training, some of us decided to visit the historical sites in and around Washington, DC. I had never visited the memorials, the Capitol Building or the White House. We took time to go to Arlington Cemetery and see President Kennedy's grave site. It was fairly new at that time. The memorial for JFK included an "eternal flame." Although I didn't voice them, my interior questions included: How was this eternal flame possible? Who maintained it? Why did they refer to it as an eternal flame? I was really curious about this eternal flame; something I had never seen before. Mystery enveloped my seeking heart. The Bible is like that never-ending flame in helping me know God. It is God's revelation of Himself, especially as unveiled in Jesus Christ. God is preaching to us about His nature and character.

Psalm 102:27 reminds me of the unfathomable side of God. The Psalmist says of God: "His years have no end." When I try to explain this hard side of knowing God to others, I feel as if I fail. Isaiah 57:15 reminds me of the long journey I am on to know what God is really like. The prophet proclaimed: "God inhabits eternity."

The apostle Paul has a parallel statement that matches these Old Testament passages. I love the Pastorals, which is what we call 1 and 2 Timothy and Titus. Paul offered this doxology in 1 Timothy 1:17. He said of our God, "To the King of the ages, immortal, invisible, the only God, be honor and glory forever and ever. Amen." He is not like me. A look in the mirror confirms reasons to laugh and then sobers us; we are dying day by day. I look forward to the New Heaven and the New Earth, and my new body. God is not like me.

#3. God is immense. I wish there were a clearer way to say this, but this is the reality that God is near and yet He is far. The word theologians use is "omnipresent." He is specifically here and yet He is everywhere. This attribute of God reminds me of Isaiah 66:1 where God says of Himself, "Heaven is my throne, and the earth is my footstool." What a picture of our Triune God! Paul preached something similar in Acts 17:28, previously mentioned, as he was speaking to philosophers and thinkers who had gathered at the Areopagus. He said of our King and Lord: "In Him we live and move and have our being...We are indeed His offspring."

Years ago, I decided to preach from the book of Jeremiah and I spent months trying to awaken the church I was serving to the size and scope of God. In the end, I simply may have exhausted that beloved local congregation, but I love the way this prophet speaks of God: "Am I a God at hand, declares the LORD, and not a God far away? Can a man hide himself in secret places so that I cannot see him?" (23:23-24). In the very next sentence, God spoke these amazing words through Jeremiah: "Do I not fill heaven and earth?" Any attempt we make to explain God's omnipresence sounds like third-grade vocabulary. How can I explain that God is not small; He is immense? I often attempt to make God small by the way I treat Him, but He is not small. My heart is cut to the quick when I think of all the times that I have dishonored God by thinking that He is like me.

#4: God is immutable. The reason I have incorporated these four "I" words is that they emphasize the incommunicable side of God—the aspects of Him that simply cannot be fully described. This fourth word, immutable, means that God is changeless. He is consistent. J.I. Packer, and other theologians like him, remind us, with very clear language, that God does not change. Our God's life, character, truth, ways, purposes and Son do not change. One of my heroes, C. S. Lewis, somewhere in his writings, said this about God: "He is the fountain of fact-hood." Lewis means that God can be counted on. Our sovereign Lord does not have ups and downs. He is not helter-skelter. Malachi 3:6 says: "For I the LORD do not change." This declarative sentence leaves no doubt about God's immutable nature. "I the Lord do not change." Hebrews 13:8 is equally clear. It is the passage where the writer says of Jesus Christ: "He is the same yesterday, today and forever." The character of God and His purpose is unchangeable (Hebrews 6:17). So, He does not waver like I do. He does not wake up cranky. He is not like me.

Understanding God's immutability is crucial to comprehending what it means to experience ongoing spiritual formation. Our understanding has hugely practical implications that we will discuss before we are done. I simply confess, again, that I don't have the words to talk about this side of God. Early in my years of teaching, I began to read Augustine's *The Confessions*. I stumbled onto what I now know is one of the most well-known paragraphs of the Bishop of Hippo. Augustine wrote:

> "Too late have I loved you, O Beauty so ancient and so new, too late have I loved you! Behold, you were within me, while I was outside: it was there that I sought you, and a deformed creature, rushed headlong upon these things of beauty which you have made. You were with me, but I was not with you. They kept me far from you, those fair things which, if they were not in you, would not exist at all. You have called to me, and have cried out, and have shattered my deafness. You have blazed forth with light, and have shone upon me, and you have put my blindness to flight! You have sent forth fragrance, and I have drawn in my breath, and I pant after you. I have tasted you, and I hunger and thirst after you. You have touched me, and I have burned for your peace."[16]

Augustine's words, and others like them, are my reminders of the grandness and glory of God. None of us can ever discover our true self until we have compared who we are to God's greatness and beauty. This is the

---
16. Augustine, *The Confessions of St. Augustine* (New York, NY: Doubleday, 1960), 254-255.

journey of a lifetime, but it is worth every step. There is none like our Triune God, three in one, in perfect harmony, Father, Son and Holy Spirit.

CHAPTER 4

THE SOUL'S LONG JOURNEY TO KNOW WHAT GOD IS LIKE: PART 2

"What type of house does the soul live in? It is a two-story house."[17]

This lifelong pilgrimage to know what God is like has a troubling temptation. We can be tempted to live solely in the physical world, only thinking of our body and thereby rejecting God, or we can be so preoccupied with the spiritual world, that we only consider the supernatural and fail to remember that God inhabits all of life. Evelyn Underhill was and is calling us to recognize that our pilgrimage to be made into the likeness of Jesus required and continues to require living in both worlds and realizing that God is sovereign over both realities. In that sense our soul is a two-story house. This common seduction of wanting to control God, or even make Him in our likeness, tripped up Israel on more than one occasion. The Old Testament story of God's people is full of this temptation to refashion God. Like Israel, many of us have been tempted to make God in our likeness.

---

17. Underhill, *Concerning the Inner Life*, 67.

God is impervious to our efforts to make Him look like you or me. Matthew Barrett is correct when he critiques our efforts. He writes:

> "God has been domesticated… Our aim, ultimately, is to know God's perfections and in so doing learn what it means to actually know God in a saving way. Only then will our affections for God be kindled… But I must warn you at the start: I will not be interested in wasting your time with a God who is tame and domesticated, a God whose divinity is humanized. That may be the God of popular culture, but it is not the God of the Bible."[18]

We must be reminded that there is a flip side to the long journey to know what God is like. The Bible is the place where we must go if we are to know the truth of who He is. Scripture does this through narrative, law, poetry, prophecy, Gospel, miracle, letter and surprisingly, through metaphor. The Bible reveals things about God through imagery. Can you answer the question: What is God like? So many passages help answer this question. Here are a few of them.

> "The LORD is a man of war" (Exodus 15:3).
>
> "Who is like you, O LORD, among the gods? Who is like you, majestic in holiness, awesome in glorious deeds, doing wonders" (Exodus 15:11)?
>
> "For the LORD your God is a consuming fire, a jealous God" (Deuteronomy 4:24).
>
> "The LORD our God, the LORD is one" (Deuteronomy 6:4).
>
> "For the LORD your God is God of gods and Lord of lords, the great, the mighty, and the awesome God, who is not partial and takes no bribe. He executes justice for the fatherless and the widow, and loves the sojourner, giving him food and clothing" (Deuteronomy 10:17-18).

---
18. Barrett, *None Greater*, 14.

> "For the LORD God is a sun and shield; the LORD bestows favor and honor. No good thing does he withhold from those who walk uprightly" (Psalm 84:11).
>
> "The LORD is the everlasting God, the Creator of the ends of the earth" (Isaiah 40:28).
>
> "And there is no other god besides me, a righteous God and a Savior; there is none besides me" (Isaiah 45:21).
>
> "For I knew that you are a gracious God and merciful, slow to anger and abounding in steadfast love, and relenting from disaster" (Jonah 4:2b).
>
> "In the beginning was the Word and the Word was with God, and the Word was God. He was in the beginning with God. All things were made through him, and without him was not anything made that was made. In him was life, and the life was the light of men" (John 1:1-4).
>
> "God is spirit, and those who worship him must worship in spirit and truth" (John 4:24).

Bible verse after Bible verse reveals what God is like. This is the communicable side of God; the side I think we can discuss over a cup of coffee. Just as there was a refined name for the previous list of God's attributes, the incommunicable or transcendent side of God, so we have a fancy name for this side of God; we call this the immanent side of God. Now and then Scripture puts these two sides of God, the transcendent side of God and the immanent side of God together. The Apostle Peter offers this example. He wrote:

> "And if you call on him as Father who judges impartially according to each one's deeds, conduct yourselves with fear throughout the time of your exile, knowing that you were ransomed from the futile ways inherited from your forefathers,

not with perishable things such as silver or gold but with the precious blood of Christ like that of a lamb without blemish or spot. He was foreknown before the foundation of the world but was made manifest in the last times for the sake of you who through him are believers in God who raised him from the dead and gave him glory so that your faith and hope are in God. Having purified your souls by your obedience to the truth for a sincere brotherly love, love one another earnestly from a pure heart, since you have been born again, not of perishable seed but of imperishable through the living and abiding word of God" (1 Peter 1:17-23).

I read that call to be holy and I am staggered by the phrase, "Before the foundation of the world." This makes it clear that God had, on His heart, the redemption, reconciliation, adoption, justification, salvation and sanctification of you and me, *before the world began*! The New Testament inserts this phrase "before the foundation of the world" eight different times (John 17:5, 17:24, Ephesians 1:4, Hebrews 4:3, 9:26, 1 Peter 1:20, Revelation 13:8 and 17:8). God purposed all of this in Christ. I don't know how to talk about this, but I must try. God did for us what we could not do for ourselves. Here, then, are five attributes of God that point to His immanent side.

#1. I know that God leads. Every believer can give an example of how God has faithfully directed their life. My own testimony is that God has led me all these years to experience Him and help others to experience Him. We experience His activity in our lives. Everyone who has said yes to Jesus has a testimony. Christ followers can look back on their journeys and see how active God was in their pre-Jesus lives. We can see that He was working in some way. Think of passages like Psalm 23:1-2, "The Lord is my shepherd, I shall not want, He makes me lie down in green pastures. He *leads* me beside still waters." Psalm 23 declares that God knows what I need long before I do, and that He will provide for me. Think of those famous texts that you may have memorized in your early steps as a Christ follower. A familiar example is Proverbs 3:5-6, "Trust in the Lord with all your heart and lean not on your own understanding. In all your ways acknowledge Him and He will direct your path." Or consider Jeremiah 29:11-13. This passage gets misused, but the fundamental idea for apprentices of Jesus is that just as God knew what would be involved in Judah's exile and seventy-year captivity in Babylon, God knows the plans He has for us. God has our best interests at heart, and He will lead us on this long journey.

Stop and consider the entire book of Genesis. As we faithfully read this first book of our Bible, at the close of Genesis 11, we are introduced to Abram or Abraham. From that point onward, God leads that patriarch day after day after day. The entire narrative of Genesis is a reminder of God's willingness to lead his people. The stories of Abraham, Isaac, Jacob (Israel) and his twelve sons, especially Joseph, testify to the truth of God's capacity and desire to lead his people. All of this "leading" talk reminds me of what I used to do when our daughters were little and prone to wander in the grocery store or the local mall. I would gently put my hands on their heads and I would steer them where I wanted them to go. Even as I recall that, I must remind myself that God is sovereign. He rules and reigns the universe, but He also gives me free will. Paradoxical. Sublime. Beautiful. He leads.

#2. I know that God longs. Each one of the incommunicable traits that I've mentioned has a counter balance. This specific attribute, that God longs for us, is the flip side to God's independence. He is independent of me, yet He still longs for me. Again, this is unexplainable unless we relate it to the way good parents feel about their children. God wants to spend time with us. God has a huge appetite for us. The reason I know that is because I have read Genesis 1 and 2. God is crazy in love with *His* children. Even when the mess of Genesis 3 enters the narrative, God still longs for fellowship with Adam and Eve. Note Ephesians 2, where Paul tells us that God in Christ broke down all the dividing walls, all the barriers between ourselves and Him and those we have with one another.

When I was a really young Christ follower, 20 years old in military service, there were these little Christian pamphlets that I would providentially discover from time to time. One of those pamphlets, written by Robert Boyd Munger, was entitled *My Heart, Christ's Home*. It told me that God in Christ longed to set up house inside of me. Munger wrote: "Without question, one of the most remarkable Christian doctrines is that Jesus Christ himself, through the presence of the Holy Spirit will actually enter a heart, settle down and be at home there. Christ will make the human heart his abode."[19] The Biblical words for that reality are "abide," "dwell," "remain." Consider John 15. Jesus said to His disciples and so He says to us, "Abide in me, and I in you" (John 15:4). He desires our company and we need His constant presence. There is a defining moment in the history of Israel, found in 2 Chronicles 16:9 where the writer says, "For the eyes of the Lord search to and fro to see whose heart is right with him." God's desire for us is real. C.S. Lewis asked us to imagine we were a living house. He described it this way:

> "God comes in to rebuild that house. At first, perhaps, you can understand what He is doing. He is getting the drains right and stopping the leaks in the roof and so on: you knew that those jobs needed doing and you are not surprised. But presently he starts knocking the house about in a way that hurts abominably and does not seem to make sense. What on earth is He up to? The explanation is that He is building quite a different house from the one you thought of, throwing out a new wing here, putting on an extra floor there, running up towers, making courtyards. You thought you were going to be made into a decent little cottage: but He is building a palace. He intends to come and live in it Himself."[20]

---

19. Robert Boyd Munger, *My Heart, Christ's Home* (Downers Grove, IL: IVP, 1975), 3.
20. Lewis, *Mere Christianity*, 160.

This promise that God longs for us is evident in Paul's prayer for the church in Ephesus. Paul prayed: "That according to the riches of his glory he may grant you to be strengthened with power through his Spirit in your inner being, so that Christ may dwell in your hearts through faith" (Ephesians 3:16-17).

#3. I know that God lingers. A third communicable side of God, the immanent side of God, is that He lingers. That means that God is ever available. Isaiah 41:10 presents this attribute simply. God said through Isaiah: "Fear not for I am with you; be not dismayed, for I am your God; I will strengthen you, I will help you, I will uphold you with my righteous hand." Even in the midst of Israel's rebellion and stubborn heart, God was available to her. Habakkuk refers to this same characteristic of God. In fact, all of Habakkuk is a wonderful reminder of God's availability. Habakkuk 3:17-19 tells us how the prophet rejoiced in God's sustaining presence, even though he was befuddled by how God could use a nation like Babylon to punish His people. Habakkuk said: "Though the fig tree should not blossom, nor fruit be on the vines, the produce of the olive fail and the fields yield no food, the flock be cut off from the fold and there be no herd in the stalls, yet I will rejoice in the LORD; I will take joy in the God of my salvation. God, the Lord, is my strength; he makes my feet like the deer's; he makes me tread on my high places." Matthew 28:18-20 also identifies this lingering attribute of God in "the Great Commission." There Jesus said, "All authority in heaven and on earth has been given to me. Go, therefore and make disciples of all nations, baptizing them in the name of the Father and of the Son and of the Holy Spirit, teaching them to observe all that I have commanded you. And behold, I am with you always to the end of the age." Do not miss Jesus' assurance, "I am with you always."

A few years back, I journeyed through my Bible and tried to identify all the passages where God made the promise that He is with us. I counted thirty-plus places. I may not have found them all, but there are many biblical promises that serve as reminders of God's abiding presence and confirm that He is a lingering God. Francis Schaeffer authored a remarkable book about this God who lingers. It is entitled *The God Who Is There.* Schaeffer was a brilliant man who ministered faithfully to a generation of college students searching for meaning in life. May the Lord bless us with theologians like Francis Schaeffer in our chaotic culture.

Decades ago, while pastoring in Champaign-Urbana, Illinois, I got a telephone call requesting that I come to one of the twin city hospitals (which no longer exists) to see a specific patient. I set aside time to see this person I had never met. Usually I stopped at the nurses' station before seeing a patient, but this time, I went directly to the room. In my hurry I did not notice the sign posted on his door. It was my first encounter with anyone who had AIDS. This was 1982 when the medical community was mystified by this disease. The young man I was there to see asked if I had noticed the sign on the door. When I said, "No," he replied that I'd better read it. I went back to the door, read the posted warning requiring anyone who entered to be masked, gowned, gloved and use precaution. After fulfilling those commands, I came back into the room and asked what he wanted to talk about. Our conversation that day was long. As I sat next to his bed, he unfolded his prodigal saga. In the end, he had questions for me: "What is God like? Can God forgive me? Can I, as a prodigal, come home? How do I know God wants to forgive me? Will he forgive me?" I affirmed to this young man what I believe that Scripture reveals about God's character. "Yes," I said, "God is a waiting Father and wants a restored relationship with you." In the next month or so, we talked several times. This young man's return to the Father was genuine as he passed from this life to the next. God lingers.

#4. I know that God lords. The fourth attribute of God is His lordship. Note the way C.S. Lewis describes this quality of God by trying to explain who Jesus really was. Lewis wrote these penetrating words:

> "I am trying here to prevent anyone saying the really foolish thing that people often say about Him: 'I'm ready to accept Jesus as a great moral teacher, but I don't accept His claim to be God.' That is the one thing we must not say. A man who was merely a man and said the sort of things Jesus said would not be a great moral teacher. He would either be a lunatic, on a level with the man who says he is a poached egg, or else he would be the Devil of Hell. You must make your choice. Either this man was, and is, the Son of God: or else a madman or something worse. You can shut Him up for a fool, you can spit at Him and kill Him as a demon; or you can fall at His feet and call Him Lord and God. But let us not come with any patronizing nonsense about His being a great human teacher. He has not left that open to us. He did not intend to."[21]

God is a dictator, albeit a benevolent one. His kingdom is not a democracy. His kingdom rule and reign are firm and universal. Psalm 139 impresses this truth. You cannot go anywhere that He is not Lord. The Psalmist asked: "Where shall I go from your Spirit? Or where shall I flee from your presence?" (139:7). Acts 2:36 underscores for all of us that our Triune God is both Lord and Christ. To put it plainly, He alone is the boss.

F. F. Bruce, one of the finest New Testament scholars of the twentieth century, wrote a little work called *The Message of the New Testament*. The fundamental thesis of that book is that Jesus is our absolute Lord. He is awesomely holy. He has no equals. We may argue about whether we think the United States is a true democracy or a federalist government, but for those of us who claim the name of Christ, we need to remember that we have one king and one king only.

---

21. Lewis, *Mere Christianity*, 40-41.

#5. I know that God loves. The final attribute of God that I want to emphasize is the fact that He loves. He cares more for us than we care for Him. John, the apostle, said it succinctly: "God is love" (1 John 4:8 and 16). He proved it by coming to us in the person of Jesus Christ and giving His life on the cross (John 3:16). C.S. Lewis described it perfectly: "The Son of God became a man to enable men to become sons of God."[22] To keep this characteristic in balance with the others, we must always remind ourselves that God is more than just this one trait. J.I. Packer said it far better than I can. He wrote:

> "God is love is not the complete truth about God so far as the Bible is concerned… The God of whom John is speaking is the God who made the world, who judged it by the Flood, who called Abraham and made of him a nation, who chastened His Old Testament people by conquest, captivity, and exile, who sent His Son to save the world, who cast off unbelieving Israel and shortly before John wrote had destroyed Jerusalem, and who would one day judge the world in righteousness. It is this God, says John, who is love."[23]

Only a God who loves does all of that. Consider Jonah. He was the most reluctant preacher who ever lived. In Jonah 1, after the prophet headed the opposite direction from Nineveh, his assigned mission field, God crafted a great fish to stop Jonah in his prophetic tracks. For three days Jonah resided in the belly of that great fish. In Matthew 12, Jesus affirmed the historical and literal reality of the Jonah story. Jesus said: "For just as Jonah was three days and three nights in the belly of the great fish, so will the Son of Man be three days and three nights in the heart of the earth" (Matthew 12:40). Ultimately, Jonah was vomited out on a beach and decided that he would submit to God's commission. He went to Nineveh and proclaimed one of the

---
22. Lewis, *Mere Christianity*, 139.
23. Packer, *Knowing God*, 108.

harshest sermons in the history of preaching: "Yet forty days, and Nineveh shall be overthrown" (Jonah 3:4)! Translated: "Repent or die!" Jonah was then frustrated and angry because the people of Nineveh actually listened, repented and fasted. They put on sackcloth, and even their livestock were covered with sackcloth. Jonah could not stomach the revival that ensued because he hated the Assyrians for what they had done to Israel. Jonah 4:2-3, cited earlier, describes the God that all Jesus followers know. Jonah, in anger, identifies God's love in action: "I knew that you are a gracious God and merciful, slow to anger and abounding in steadfast love, and relenting from disaster. Therefore now, O LORD, please take my life from me, for it is better for me to die than to live." Consider John 3:16, Romans 5:8 and Ephesians 1:5. 1 John 3:1 is a great reminder of the loving nature of God: "See what kind of love the Father has given to us that we should be called children of God; and so we are."

E. Stanley Jones, the great missionary to India, said if God had a favorite word, it would be "come." God invites us to Himself because He loves us. There is something mind-blowing about placing the unknowing side of God, the transcendent side of God, alongside the knowing side of God, the immanent side of God. Only as we see God in all of His glorious nature do we begin to have a robust view of who He is and what He is like. For the believer, it takes a lifetime to begin to capture the nuances, what we would call the attributes, the characteristics, the traits of God. So, the fundamental question that we need to consider is this: What kind of God do you really know?

I encounter people all the time who may not know the biblical story, but through their words, describe the God they know as much like the ancient Egyptian Pharaoh who commanded the taskmasters of enslaved Israel: "You shall no longer give the people straw to make bricks, as in the past; let them go and gather straw for themselves. But the number of bricks that they made in the past you shall impose on them, you shall by no means reduce it, for they are idle" (Exodus 5:7-8). Such people hear God saying to them, "I want you to work hard at this relationship with me, I want you to make spiritual bricks, but you've got to find your own straw. Whatever you do, you must meet my expectations." Relating that kind of God is not sustainable. I have used the words of C.S. Lewis to define what it truly means to be a Jesus follower, to be someone who knows what God is really like. Lewis observed:

> "A Christian is not a man (or woman) who never goes wrong, but a man who is enabled to repent and pick himself up and begin over again after each stumble, because the Christ-life is inside him, repairing him all the time, enabling him to repent… That is why the Christian is in a different position from other people who are trying to be good. They hope, by being good, to please God if there is one; or, if they think there is not, at least they hope to deserve approval from good men. But the Christian thinks any good he does comes from the Christ-life inside of him. He does not think God will love us because we are good, but that God will make us good because He loves us… "[24]

I find no better words to end this part of our long journey to know God than those of J.I. Packer. He said:

> "What matters supremely, therefore, is not, in the last analysis, the fact that I know God, but the larger fact which underlies it, the fact that He knows me. I am graven on the palms of His hands. I am never out of His mind. All my knowledge of Him depends on His sustained initiative in knowing me. I know Him, because He first knew me and continues to know me. He knows me as a friend, one who loves me; and there is no moment when His eye is off me, or His attention distracted from me, and no moment, therefore, when His care falters."[25]

---

24. Lewis, *Mere Christianity*, 49.
25. Packer, *Knowing God*, 37.

It is my enormous joy and may it be yours to press on in this pilgrimage "looking forward to the city that has foundations, whose designer and builder is God" (Hebrews 11:10). Our soul's house is portable.

CHAPTER 5

FORMATION'S HOUSE BUILDER: ESSENTIAL FOUNDATIONAL WORK

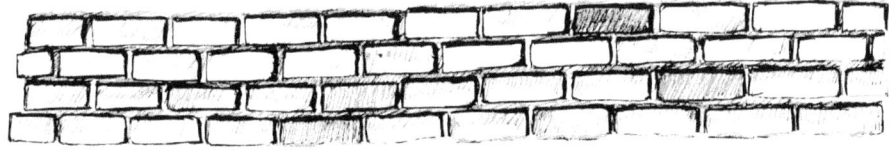

> *"If the house is to be well run, we must begin by cleaning the kitchen and the scullery; and giving their energetic but unruly inhabitants their jobs."*[26]

God the Holy Spirit takes the initiative. He is the builder of the house of the soul. Evelyn Underhill described it this way. She wrote the premise upon which this book is written: "The soul's house, that interior dwelling-place which we all possess, for the upkeep of which we are responsible, a place in which we can meet God, or from which in a sense we can exclude God, that is not too big an idea for us."[27] I want to help each of us build a God-honoring spiritual house. As noted in the definition, this construction and maintenance happens through various means. There are many avenues through which this building, or as the theologians say, sanctification, takes place. I want to identify four. Think of these four as house cleaning or renovation tools.

---

26. Underhill, *Concerning the Inner Life*, 75.
27. Ibid., 65.

The first of these means that the Holy Spirit uses to form us into Christlikeness is the practice of incorporating **spiritual disciplines** or **Christian exercises** into our everyday life. I am more comfortable with the language of John Wesley and others like him who have named these disciplines or exercises "holy habits." I acknowledge, in my own journey, that the holy habits have been the single greatest tool that God has used in cleaning up my soul's house. We must remember from the start that any practice that incorporates holy habits into our everyday life cannot save us. Only God saves through Jesus Christ. The habits cannot transform us. Again, only God the Spirit does that. What the holy habits *can* do is serve as God's transportation system. The steady and faithful incorporation of holy habits brings us into God's loving presence where He does the changing, the necessary cleaning. I will unpack the significance of this following a slight but important detour.

I believe that a holy habit can defeat an unholy habit. My early years were blanketed with a propensity toward swearing, especially when I was angry at someone or something. Only as I became a Christ follower and began to memorize Scripture did my tendency for cussing in angry moments come under the control of the Holy Spirit. He used the Word in my heart to control the emotions that surfaced in my mouth. God the Spirit, as the years have passed since my conversion, has cleaned up my vocabulary by replacing it with the language of the Scriptures.

There are three holy habits that I believe are nonnegotiable. These three are Word intake, prayer intimacy and worship intensity. Not one of us will get very far in the Jesus-following life without the regular practice of these spiritual exercises. Let's start with **Word intake**. There is no ongoing transformation apart from the Holy Spirit using Scripture in our lives. If we are to have a healthy interior world, we must maintain this first holy habit. What you do with the Word and how you practice absorbing it into your life will primarily be based upon your personality. For some of us our Word intake might be digitally driven. Many of us have iPhones that give us access to Bible apps that will read Scripture to us. Others of us prefer reading our Bibles to ourselves. There is no one way to practice this holy habit. I prefer reading my Bible systematically through a yearly reading plan, but not all of us are wired that way. If we are to have a well-maintained soul house, one that is not messy or slummy, the Scriptures are a central and necessary ingredient. So we hear, read, memorize, meditate and obey the Scriptures as part of our everyday habits.

Second, **prayer intimacy** is also a crucial daily practice. It is necessary, because all of us need to stay in touch with our heavenly headquarters. Prayer intimacy is as much listening to the Father's voice and allowing Him to guide us, as it is talking with Him and asking for His help. Prayer is an ongoing conversation. God has spoken and speaks through His Word and we listen. We then respond to God, based on that Word, and God listens. Prayer is an ongoing conversation that started with God's Word and grace and continues as intimate communion between ourselves and Him. The Scriptures teach us the significance of prayer. In the Bible, we have at least 50 lengthy prayers, not including the 150 found in the Psalms, and hundreds of smaller prayers scattered throughout its pages. Tim Keller says it so well. He writes: "Prayer is so great that wherever you look in the Bible, it is there. Why? Everywhere God is, prayer is. Since God is everywhere and infinitely great, prayer must be all-pervasive in our lives."[28] How or in whatever way we choose to pray, all of us need daily prayer practice morning, noon, and night. What our personal prayer patterns are will depend greatly upon how God created us to communicate, but may we grow into unceasing prayer intimacy with our Lord (1 Thessalonians 5:17).

The third non-negotiable holy habit is **worship intensity**. This certainly

---

28. Tim Keller, *Prayer: Experiencing Awe and Intimacy with God* (New York, NY: Penguin Books, 2014), 28.

includes gathering with the Body of Christ on Sunday, but worship is not a once-a-week habit. True and sincere worship is often public, but also necessary in our private times with God. We may have different concepts when we hear the word "worship," but I like the plain way Donald Whitney describes this practice. He writes:

> "To worship God is to ascribe the proper worth to God, to magnify His worthiness of praise, or better, to approach and address God as He is worthy… If you could see God at this moment, you would so utterly understand how worthy He is of worship that you would instinctively fall on your face and worship Him. That's why we read in Revelation that those around the throne who see Him fall on their faces in worship and those creatures closest to Him are so astonished with His worthiness that throughout eternity they ceaselessly worship Him with the response of 'Holy, holy, holy.' So worship is focusing on and responding to God… Worship often includes words and actions, but it goes beyond them to the focus of the mind and heart. Worship is the God-centered focus and response of the inner man; it is being preoccupied with God."[29]

Your response to what Donald Whitney writes will be dictated by how God has wired you. This regular private time of worship may include music or it may not. If it does, this holy habit might involve playing worship music and singing along or it might include using an old hymnal and singing to our King. This practice of worship intensity may include the use of our body as our worship instrument. We may sit before Him, stand before Him, kneel before Him, bow our heads before Him, prostrate ourselves before Him, clap our hands to Him, lift our arms to Him and use our bodies as each one of us

---

29. Donald Whitney, *Spiritual Disciplines for the Christian Life* (Colorado Springs, CO: NavPress, 1991), 81-82.

finds meaningful ways to praise our Creator and Savior. He is worthy.

Long ago, as I was beginning to understand that the Psalms could be an integral part of my ongoing formation and daily worship practice, I was struck by the various ways the writers spoke of their bodies. They wrote of standing before the Lord, lifting hands, clapping hands, kneeling, bowing, laying oneself before the Lord, and raising the head heavenward with open eyes. I was inspired by how active their worship was. It is these engaging descriptions of worship practice that I want to emulate daily for my King's honor.

So, when I think of the disciplines, I think of these three primarily, but there are many more. If you are familiar with Adele Ahlberg Calhoun's *Spiritual Disciplines Handbook* (Revised Edition), you know that she describes eighty-five different holy habits that we can practice. Adele's beautiful, remarkable and readable book is the most comprehensive guide I have read and I highly recommend it.

Holy habits are only one of the means the Holy Spirit uses in our ongoing formation, but there is a second means that many of us have found just as helpful. Think of the impact and influence that **sacred friendships** have played in our transformation, and how they have encouraged our Jesus-following life. Many of us can testify about how the right person, entering our life at the right time and speaking the right word, helped form us more and more into Christ's likeness. It is God's grace that He uses these Jesus-saturated friendships. There is something about sacred companions that are indispensable to our formation. God has not called us to live this life alone—He calls us into His community as Jesus' apprentices. I am more comfortable with a smaller group, but some of you love the crowds. This is another example of God's creativity in creating each one of us. Stop right now and recall the mentors, the coaches, the key people who have come along at just the right time and encouraged your walk with Jesus, and praise Him!

Every time I lean into this particular means of spiritual formation, my mind returns to Heyworth, Illinois and my third-grade teacher, Mrs. Yates. She was a godly woman, a genuine Christ follower who had the capacity to speak the right word, at the right time, in the right way. She would prophesy over me, saying, "I know tomorrow when you come back to school you are going to be on your best behavior. You will be ready for that math test as well." Her words became my desire. I believed that she loved me and wanted the best for me, so I simply did my part because I knew she cared for me. She was a profound voice in my life. I particularly recall the field trip we took to the local drugstore at the end of the school year. To demonstrate a lesson about the economy and business, she said one of us could write out the check to pay for the treats we had that day. She chose me for that high privilege and I've never forgotten it. Today Mrs. Yates would probably use a digital tool to teach us about money and business, but her favor to me that day was immeasurably gracious and a mark of transformation in my life. Mrs. Yates died years ago, but I still remember clearly the kindness she showed me and the hunger she instilled within me for learning.

The third means the Holy Spirit uses to change us into Jesus' likeness is **time**. When I consider this specific means, I always find myself coming back to Miles Stanford's classic and concise book, *The Green Letters: Principles of Spiritual Growth.* It offers eighteen superb essays that are reflections on growing in Christ. The second essay is labeled "Time." I cherish Stanford's insightful words. He wrote:

> "It seems that most believers have difficulty in realizing and facing up to the inexorable fact that God does not hurry in His development of our Christian life. He is working from and for eternity… Since the Christian life matures and becomes fruitful by the principle of growth (2 Peter 3:18), rather than by struggle and 'experiences,' much time is involved. A.H. Strong illustrated

it for us: A student asked the President of his school whether he could not take a shorter course than the one prescribed. 'Oh yes,' replied the President, 'but then it depends upon what you want to be. When God wants to make an oak, He takes a hundred years, but when He wants to make a squash, He takes six months.' Let's settle it once and for all, there are no shortcuts to reality… Unless the time factor is acknowledged from the heart, there is always danger of turning to the false enticement of a shortcut… Spiritual renewal is a gradual process. All growth is progressive, and the finer the organism, the longer the process. It is from measure to measure… It is from stage to stage."[30]

Stanford's point is my point. Time is essential to our ongoing spiritual formation. Paul said so in Philippians 1:6. He understood the nature of Christian maturity and the time involved. He wrote: "And I am sure of this, that he who began a good work in you will bring it to completion at the day of Jesus Christ." Time is a critical component to our maturation. Transformation cannot be hurried or microwaved. A marathon of faithfulness is required. I particularly love Eugene Peterson's phrase borrowed from the writings of Nietzsche. The Christ-following life calls for "a long obedience in the same direction." The Holy Spirit takes the long view. Time is required.

The fourth and final means that is an essential foundation work on our soul's house is something others before me have called **providential circumstances.** This is the means the Spirit uses when suffering, pain, heartache, and disappointment enter our lives. No one escapes them. In these times, whether we surrender to the Spirit at work in it or defy Him makes all the difference. As you testify to your own formative life in Christ, you then can share, "I grew enormously in that season of suffering. I would not want to repeat it, but I see God's transforming hand in it. It was both awful and wonderful."

---

30. Miles Stanford, "Time," in *The Green Letters: Principles of Spiritual Growth* (Grand Rapids, MI: Zondervan, 1975), 13-15.

Whenever I think about this fourth means, I find myself considering the New Testament letter of James. James uses two magnificent key words, with three unique implications, to describe the unavoidable pain that comes knocking at the door of our life experiences. First, the enemy of our soul enters to *tempt* us (*peirazo*). James wrote: "Let no one say when he is *tempted*, 'I am being *tempted* by God,' for God cannot be *tempted* with evil, and he himself *tempts* no one. But each person is *tempted* when he is lured and enticed by his own desire" (James 1:13-14). All believers experience this. 1 Corinthians 10:13 assures us: "No *temptation* has overtaken you that is not common to man. God is faithful, he will not let you be *tempted* beyond your ability, but with the *temptation* he will also provide the way of escape that you may be able to endure it." *Temptations* are a result of living in a world that is ruled by Satan. Even our Savior was not permitted to bypass that. Think Matthew 4, Luke 4, and hints of this in Mark 1. *Temptations* are the result of an enemy who roams the universe and works against the purpose and plan of God.

The second word that James shared to remind us of providential circumstances and how God alone can use them as a transforming means is the word *"trials"* (*peirasmos*). You might have noticed that the same Greek root word is used for both being *tempted* and enduring *trials*. James said, "Count it all joy, my brothers, when you meet *trials* of various kinds… Blessed is the man who remains steadfast under *trial*" (James 1:2 and 12). *Trials* are the result of living in a world that has been wrecked by sin. Nobody evades these heart wrenching experiences. An example that may come across as vulgar and crass, but that makes my point is that as small groups use our church building to meet; if I were to snoop in the parking lot, I would find a car with a bumper sticker that declares, "S**t happens." That is inappropriate and inarticulate, but it comes close to what James meant by a *trial*. Bad things happen because we live in a sin-wrecked world.

The last word that James used mystifies me. He calls it a *"test"* (*dokimion*). The word used by James implies a proof or a chance to prove something. He wrote: "For you know that the *testing* of your faith produces steadfastness. And let steadfastness have its full effect, that you may be perfect and complete, lacking in nothing… For when he has stood the *test* he will receive the crown of life, which God has promised to those who love him" (James 1:3 and 12). *Tests* are the result of God loving us so much that there is no other way to deepen our spiritual roots except to take us through a season of *testing*.

Genesis 22:1 is the first place in the Scriptures where "*test*" is inserted. The text says, "God *tested* Abraham." God said to Abraham, "Take your son, your only son Isaac, whom you love, and go to the land of Moriah, and offer him there as a burnt offering on one of the mountains of which I shall tell you" (22:2). I struggle to fathom the divine plan behind all of this. Abraham obeyed. I am confident three sleepless nights followed. On the third day Abraham came to the place God has chosen. Abraham did all the preparatory work required. Just as was he about to use the knife to kill his own son, God stopped him and graciously provided a ram in Isaac's place. This grief was averted, but more *tests* came Abraham's way.

Throughout Scripture there appear to be seasons of *testing*. Here is the unanswerable question: How do I know which word from James is happening in my life? Is this a *temptation, trial* or *test*? I confess that I cannot always tell. In hindsight, I sometimes find clarity. I look back and I remind myself that my experience was the result of living in a world that has been fractured by sin. That is a trial. Maybe as I look back, I recognize my own duplicity. I yielded to a *temptation* from the enemy and it brought heartache into my life. I do not always know what God is doing. I *do* know that in the God-soaked circumstances that come into my life, in the "all things" of my life, the Triune God providentially controls and works "together for good, for those who are called according to his purpose" (Romans 8:28).

God the Holy Spirit takes the initiative through various means. He is formation's Builder and He does the essential foundation work. The means He uses include holy habits, time, sacred friendships, providential circumstances and more. In the end, I come back to the wise words of Evelyn Underhill. She said:

> "Don't confuse your meals with your life, and your clothes with your body. Don't lose your head over what perishes. Nearly everything does perish: so face the facts, don't rush after the transient and unreal. Maintain your soul in tranquil dependence on God, don't worry; don't mistake what you possess for what you are. Accumulating things is useless... The simpler your house, the easier it will be to run."[31]

I will have more to say about that later. For now, I believe the formation's Builder knows best.

---

31. Underhill, *Concerning the Inner Life*, 92.

CHAPTER 6

WORKING ALONGSIDE THE MASTER HOUSE BUILDER

> *"There is not one landlord for the lower floor, and another for the upstairs flat… The landlord of the upper floor is the landlord of the ground floor too."*[32]

The soul's house is our Lord's if we are truly Christ followers. We work alongside Him. We are always being formed. Rich Villodas expresses it well. He writes:

> "Whether we know it or not, see it or not, or understand it or not, we are always at risk of being shallowly formed. We are formed by our false selves, our families of origin, the highly manipulated presentations of social media and the value system of the world that determines worth based on accomplishments, possessions, efficiency, intellectual acumen, and gifts. So we need to be regularly called back to the essence of our lives in God. That essence is one of ongoing transformation; that is, Christ being formed in us."[33]

---
32. Underhill, *Concerning the Inner Life*, 76.
33. Rich Villodas, *The Deeply Formed Life* (Colorado Springs, CO: WaterBrook Books, 2020), xv.

There are two key formational New Testament words that come to mind when I consider what it means to work alongside our Triune God, the Master Builder, in the ongoing renovation of our inner house. Those two New Testament Greek verbs are *askeo* and *gumnazo*. *Askeo* is the word "exercise." It means to take great pain and effort to train to do something worthwhile. *Askeo* implies entering into a regimen of discipline to win a prize. *Askeo* is from the root word that I have already mentioned: ascetic. This first word paints a picture of someone who repeatedly practices certain exercises in order to reach a high level of skill. Paul used this word in Acts 24:16. He said: "So I always *take pains* to have a clear conscience toward both God and man." Through training and discipline, Paul became skillful in using his God-given conscience. There is an appropriate place for us to think of regular, rhythmic, spiritual exercise. Often, in the midst of this spiritual exercising, we find ourselves coming back to the holy habits and other means that we have talked about previously.

The second formational word is the verb *gumnazo*. It literally means to go to the gymnasium. Paul used this word twice in 1 Timothy 4:7-8. He wrote: "Have nothing to do with irreverent, silly myths. Rather *train* yourself for godliness, for while bodily *training* is of some value, godliness is of value in every way, as it holds promise for the present life and also for the life to come." Originally, in Ancient Greece, this word was used to describe someone who exercised naked. The New Testament writers used this word to portray something distinctively different. There, an athlete of God is a disciple of Jesus, one who trains his or her body and mind to know the difference between good and evil and ultimately brings glory to God.

I bring attention to these two New Testament words because there must be an intentionality in our Jesus-following life. We don't drift into Christian maturity or ongoing spiritual formation. There must be a resolved mindset, a resolution of the heart to work alongside the Master Builder in the soul's house. Questions must be asked. Is your mind made up to grow into the man or woman God desires? Is your heart set on maturing into Jesus' likeness? Again, I return to Evelyn Underhill's *words*. She wrote:

> "God comes to the soul in His working clothes, and brings His tools with Him. We need fortitude if we are to accept with quietness the sharp blows and persistent sandpapering which bring our half-finished fitments up to the standard required by the city's plan… It is not a week-end cottage. It must be planned and organized for life, the whole of life, not for fine weather alone. Hence strong walls and dry cellars matter more than many balconies or interesting garden design."[34]

Our spiritual exercising and training matter. Our cooperation with God the Spirit is vital, but if anyone thinks that I have somehow mistakenly slipped into talking about earning salvation or practicing sanctification as a do-it-yourself project, I will let Underhill speak again. She correctly reminds all of us of the centrality and dependency we must have on our Master Builder. Underhill's small, but important book, *The Spiritual Life,* is the perfect reminder. Evelyn wrote:

> "For a spiritual life is simply a life in which all that we do comes from the centre, where we are anchored in God: a life soaked through and through by a sense of His reality and claim, and self-give to the great movement of His will… He alone matters, He alone is. Our spiritual life is His affair, because, whatever we may think to the contrary, it is really produced by His steady attraction, and our humble and self-forgetful response to it."[35]

God's toolbox is immense. His work and initiative are required.

---
34. Underhill, *Concerning the Inner Life*, 100.
35. Evelyn Underhill, *The Spiritual Life* (Harrisburg, PA: Morehouse Publishing, 1994), 32, 35.

His toolbox holds all the necessary tools for our ongoing formation and apprenticeship. All of this reminds me of my toolbox that I keep in my garage. My wife found it for me at one of those neighborhood garage sales. Someone's discarded toolbox became my toolbox treasure. I love that red, four-drawer, rolling Craftsman tool chest that Sears sold for years. I keep all my motorcycle tools in it. Sometimes I think I'm a big shot because I have this great toolbox. But the truth of the matter is clear; I don't always know how to use some of the tools that I own. I sometimes need help. God's divine toolbox makes mine look like a child's toy box and only He knows how to use all of His tools. His tools have eternal implications etched upon them. Consider these important questions: Do you gravitate toward a particular spiritual tool? If so, which one? How has God used that tool or any of His tools in the building of your soul's house? What has God taught you about working alongside Him in the maintenance of your interior home?

A few of you may have read my reading primer, *Reading With God in Mind*. One of the key principles of that book is the importance of finding books or authors who can help encourage and mentor us. When we find an author who speaks our heart language, we tend to read everything that person has written. That writer becomes a grace-filled gift to us. I don't know how to explain that miracle, except to note that its occurrence is providential. That author becomes a lifelong friend who shows up at our soul's house from time to time and offers a helping hand in our continual transformation.

A couple of years ago our youngest daughter surprised us and bought us concert tickets to hear Andrea Bocelli perform at the Rosemont in Chicago. My wife and I made the two-hour drive, located our seats and for the first two-thirds of Bocelli's performance, I struggled to pay attention. I do not have a trained ear for opera. Opera is not my preferred music genre. Sue, though, loved it. I watched her lean into the music and listen attentively to Bocelli's voice. The intermission arrived and I truly thought about bolting, but I watched with interest when Andrea was helped off the stage by an assistant. I was reminded of his story. Bocelli, like most of us, was born with the ability to see. A soccer accident, a blow to his head, blinded him and altered his life.

Following the intermission, Bocelli returned to the stage and began to sing in English. He performed songs that I knew, understood and appreciated, rather than Italian opera selections. He sang "The Prayer," "Time to Say Goodbye," "I Believe," and others. I found myself weeping. I had never thought of music and Bocelli as participants in the building of my inner life, but I found myself inspired and more eager to be all that my King desired me to be. On our way home, it was like the experience of the two on the road to Emmaus. Jesus joined us in our car and as we drove, we reflected on how the music inspired and healed our souls. God's toolbox is deep enough, sturdy enough, and organized enough that He can use the exact tool that is needed, at any moment. He is the Master Builder.

Because our Triune God is the Master Builder, I want to clarify how we work alongside Him in the building of the house of the soul. What is involved? I believe that there are at least four answers.

The first and most obvious requirement of this inner construction project is that it demands **a personal response to God and a desire to walk in His Spirit.** This may sound like Sunday school 101, but it is foundational that a personal decision has been made, that Jesus Christ has been received as Lord and Savior, and that His completed work on the cross has been accepted. It means that I believe that in Christ alone I find salvation. It means that I believe and affirm the very words of Peter when he went before the Jerusalem council and proclaimed: "And there is salvation in no one else, for there is no other name under heaven given among men by which we must be saved" (Acts 4:12). A saving work in the heart must be done before building can begin.

If I were to go to my local Barnes and Noble and look at the religion or spirituality section, I would be hard pressed to find resources, other than the Bible, that are grounded firmly in a Christ-centered worldview. I would find a variety of volumes that would include Muslim, Hindu, or Eastern spirituality; whole schools of thought that advocate self-improvement or explain how to save oneself. In a Christ-centered worldview, the contrast is startling. There is the recognition that there is a King, a sovereign King of the universe who invites us into a relationship with Him. It is by grace, through faith, that we respond to this King and walk according to His kingdom's way. When I think of what it means to build alongside of Him, this personal response is the first answer that we must give.

The second answer that comes to mind is this: Working alongside the Master Builder requires **recognizing the presence of God's grace in every area of my life**. Grace always. What is uniquely Christian is that grace not only saves us, but grace also sanctifies us. The grace of our Triune God permeates everything about the life I want to build. For a time, I studied with Richard Foster at Friends University in Wichita, Kansas. Richard would come into class and say this one thing time after time. "The grace of God is at work every day. Why don't we see it more?" Then he would lovingly reproach us about our lack of alertness, watchfulness and awareness of the permeating grace of God in all of reality. Recognizing the presence of the grace of God in every area of our life is fundamental to cooperating with Him in the enterprise of building an inner life suitable for His indwelling. A.W. Tozer called what I am attempting to describe "spiritual receptivity." He said:

> "I venture to suggest that the one vital quality which they (the great saints) had in common was spiritual receptivity. Something in them was open to heaven, something which urged them Godward… They had spiritual awareness and that they went on

to cultivate it until it became the biggest thing in their lives… Receptivity is not a single thing; rather, it is a compound, a blending of several elements within the soul… It may be increased by exercise or destroyed by neglect. It is not a sovereign and irresistible force which comes upon us as a seizure from above. It is a gift of God, indeed, but one which must be recognized and cultivated as any other gift if we are to realize the purpose for which it was given."[36]

Christian spiritual formation is unique, even paradoxical, in that it is not my effort that builds the house of the soul. It is all grace.

The third response involved in partnering with the Master Builder requires **working cooperatively with God's purposes, both privately and corporately.** It includes my own intentionality, as well as the intentionality of the Christian community with whom I identify. I have grown heartsick over what I hear often these days. It is the warped, even heretical view that announces, "I love Christ, but I hate the church." I was running a little late and hurrying into a University of Illinois football game a few years ago with my son-in-law and my grandson. We were required to pass through a security checkpoint, and in our haste, I barely noticed a young man standing near the checkpoint entrance holding a huge sign. The sign said, "I love Jesus, but '*F*' the church." I was anxious to get into the stadium, and had almost decided to walk past the sign holder, but I found myself telling Matt, my son-in-law, that I was going to go back and talk to him if he would talk with me. I asked Matt to take Preston in and get our seats and I would follow as soon as I could. Just as I turned around to start a conversation with this young man, the police were removing him. That young man's sign epitomized what many people express today. "Yes, I love Jesus; Jesus is great, but the church… I don't want anything to do with the church." The thought of separating Jesus from His church would have never entered the

---

36. A.W. Tozer, *The Pursuit of God* (Camp Hill, PA: Christian Publications, 1982), 67-69.

minds of the New Testament contributors. To work alongside the Master Builder requires that I tether myself to His church, warts and all. He requires that I love and serve His bride.

My fourth and final implication as to what it means to work alongside the Master Builder is this: I am required to **keep Jesus at the center of my life.** Christian spiritual formation assumes nothing less than this. Jesus must be at the center of every part of my life. There was a time when I thought I wanted to engage in theology at the doctoral level. For a brief summer, I was a student at Southern Baptist Seminary in Louisville, Kentucky. I was treated well, but there was a great deal of disagreement in those days regarding Scripture's inerrancy. I was in a summer class studying the theology of Karl Barth with Dr. David Mueller. Mueller had studied with Barth. Dr. Mueller was waxing eloquent during one of those long summer afternoons when I heard an unforgettable sentence. Mueller said, "When the center is correct, the circumference takes care of itself." The genesis of that statement is found in Barth's discussion on the supremacy of Christ in his *Dogmatics in Outline*. When Christ saturates the very essence of the church, everything else finds its proper place. This is precisely what my fourth point requires. I want to maintain Jesus at the center of all that I do, all that I am, all that I say. He is the landlord of my soul's house.

I once made a passing comment to one of my adult students, Beth Cash. I said to Beth, "I love coffee, particularly a coffee out of Louisville called John Conte. I especially enjoy their chocolate raspberry blend." Soon after, there was a ring at our door and a huge basket from the John Conte Coffee Company was delivered. The company that Beth worked for had Conte as one of their clients. I even received a phone call from someone at John Conte asking me, "How do you like the coffee?" I was completely flabbergasted and I don't remember ever feeling more privileged. Beth blessed me through a simple act of selflessness. Beth and her husband, Eric, are kind-hearted and gracious people, and decided, "We can bless JK with coffee that he loves and we want to do that." So I was on the receiving end of a John Conte coffee blessing. In ways that are beyond comprehension, God the Master House Builder has decided to bless me and all Christ followers with "every spiritual blessing in the heavenly places, even as he chose us in him before the foundation of the world, that we should be holy and blameless before him" (Ephesians 1:3-4). All because God decided to build a house inside of me where Christ could dwell in my heart through faith and let me work alongside Him, the Master Builder.

CHAPTER 7

THE READING ROOM IN THE SOUL'S HOUSE

"If the house is to be a success, what we leave out will be quite as important as what we put in."[37]

Evelyn Underhill was right. What we leave out and what we put in our soul's house makes all the difference. I remind all of us that God is the builder of our soul's house, but we play a significant role in choosing accessories, furniture, flooring, colors and books. Everyone who seeks to live in a proper house of the soul should have a designated reading room. The decision to put God at the center of our reading is paramount to the soul. Eugene Peterson's *Eat This Book* is one of my favorite works of his. In it, Peterson shares that one of the first metaphors for writing and reading that struck him was one from Kafka: "If the book we are reading does not wake us, as with a fist hammering on our skull, why then do we read it?… A book must be like an ice axe to break the frozen sea within us."[38] Reading is essential to the building and maintenance of the soul. Peterson, a few pages later in his

---

37. Underhill, *Concerning the Inner Life*, 87.
38. Eugene Peterson, *Eat This Book* (Grand Rapids, MI: Eerdmans, 2006), 8. As quoted by George Steiner. *Language and Silence* (New York, NY: Atheneum, 1970), 67.

book, inserted this small, but mighty sentence: "Reading is an immense gift, but only if the words are assimilated, taken into the soul—eaten, chewed, gnawed, received in unhurried delight."[39] Peterson was specifically speaking about Scripture reading and Peterson's method needs to be employed in any kind of reading that causes us to read with God in mind.

We begin, then, by asking an important question. What is the theological foundation for using reading in this building project? Three answers will suffice. First, God Himself uses and is the creator of language. He spoke the written Word into existence. The things that He wants us to understand about who He is, His nature, His activity, His purpose, His plan—all of these, He spoke into comprehensible language. He wants us to know Him. This is fundamental to understanding the necessity of having a reading room in our soul's home. There is nothing we read that could have been written without our Triune God's desire to communicate with words. I recognize the sobering reality that much of what we can read is not good and godly, yet I believe that God will one day reclaim and repair all language.

Second, Jesus is the incarnate Word. He put on flesh and became for us the Living Word. John 1:1-2 and 1:14 tell us so. John wrote: "In the beginning was the Word, and the Word was with God, and the Word was God. He was in the beginning with God… And the Word became flesh and dwelt among us, and we have seen His glory, glory as of the only Son, from the Father, full of grace and truth." Jesus is that Word. In addition, Colossians 1:17-18 magnificently reminds us that this same Word is "before all things, and in him all things hold together. And he is the head of the body, the church. He is the beginning, the firstborn from the dead, that in everything he might be preeminent." Jesus is the central subject of all of our reading.

Reading matters. Theologically speaking, God spoke the Word, Jesus is the Word and the Holy Spirit still speaks the Word to us in a variety of

---

39. Peterson, *Eat This Book*, 11.

ways. This voice of the Holy Spirit is the third foundational call to read with God in mind. Hebrews 3:7-8 explodes with significance. The passage reads: "Therefore, as the Holy Spirit says, 'Today if you hear His voice, do not harden your hearts as in the rebellion, on the day of testing, in the wilderness.'" The author of Hebrews, several chapters later, repeats this idea. He writes: "And the Holy Spirit also bears witness to us; for after saying, 'This is the covenant that I will make with them after those days, declares the Lord: I will put my laws on their hearts and write them on their minds,' then He adds, 'I will remember their sins and their lawless deeds no more'" (Hebrews 10:15-17). The Holy Spirit speaks the Word deeply and intimately into our heart through our reading.

So, how do we respond to these theological foundations? What do we do in terms of creating a reading room for the soul's house? What suggestions will be helpful? I'll share here what I wrote some twenty years ago in *Reading With God in Mind*. I offer seven encouragements to help in the establishment of our soul's reading house.

First, **we should always look at the Scriptures as the foundation and core of all our reading.** Let us measure all of our reading by the Word. What God has revealed in His Word must become the final authority for everything. I read widely. I hope you do. But if the Bible does not have first place in our reading, then the snares of the enemy will trip us. The wise J.I. Packer wrote:

> "If I were the devil, one of my first aims would be to stop folk from digging into the Bible. Knowing that it is the Word of God, teaching (people) to know and love and serve the God of the Word, I should do all I could to surround it with the spiritual equivalent of pits, thorn hedges, and man traps, to frighten people off… At all costs I should want to keep them from using their minds in a disciplined way to get the measure of its message."[40]

---

40. J.I. Packer, *Knowing Scripture* (Downers Grove, IL: IVP, 1979), 9-10.

Scripture reading must ever and always be our priority. Donald Whitney raised the perfect question. He asked: "If your growth in Godliness were measured by the quality of your Bible intake, what would be the result? This is an important question, for the truth is, your growth in Godliness is greatly affected by the quality of your Bible intake."[41]

Second, **we should ask God to lead us to the books that He would have us read.** I do not know if you feel the same stress I do about choosing the right book. Brilliant Alan Jacobs points out the anxiety that many of us encounter in selecting what we read even as we ache for tranquility. Jacobs writes: "Some therapists who work with young people today say that the single greatest source of stress and anxiety for them is the sheer number of *choices* they have before them, which generates the fear that if they make the wrong choices they may not be able to get over their own errors. And my long experience as a teacher confirms this interpretation."[42] My friend Jackina Stark, who taught for years at Ozark Christian College, gave me a word of grace and reminded me that when I feel overwhelmed by the number of books available, I could pray her brother's prayer. He would pray: "Lord, what books do you want me to read? There are too many. Lead me to the right ones." Stephen Um, in his helpful commentary on 1 Corinthians, encourages me to pray similarly. He affirms the staggering amount of information overload that exists in our time. There are just too many books to read. Um writes:

> "Currently, the Library of Congress houses eighteen million books. American publishers add another two hundred thousand titles to this stack each year. This means that at the current publishing rate, ten million new books will be added in the next fifty years. Add together the dusty LOC volumes with the shiny new and

---

41. Donald Whitney, *Spiritual Disciplines for the Christian Life*, 33.
42. Alan Jacobs, *Breaking Bread With The Dead: A Reader's Guide to a More Tranquil Mind* (New York, NY: Penguin Press, 2020), 5.

forthcoming books, and you get a bookshelf-warping total of twenty-eight million books available for an English reader in the next fifty years! But you can read only 2,000–because you are a wildly ambitious book devourer… For every one book that you choose to read, you must ignore ten thousand other books simply because you don't have the time."[43]

The writer of Ecclesiastes echoes this reality to all who listen. Ecclesiastes 12:12 says, "Of making many books there is no end, and much study is a weariness of the flesh." I have several reading practices that I place next to this prayer and these simple habits help me discern my next book to read. One of those elementary practices is asking people I know and love what they are reading. I also receive digital catalogues and new book announcements from Christian publishers that I trust. I pay attention to the footnotes in the books that I read, and often those footnotes will lead me to my next book. I encourage all of us to be footnote watchers.

Dr. Rob Maupin, a beloved brother in Christ, brought words of grace to me years ago. Rob and I connected when he was an undergraduate student, and then reconnected years later as fellow professors. I love Rob and his precious family. He noticed how burdened I felt about the number of books I could not find the time to read. Rob said to me, "I would like to give you a grace gift. You don't have to read every book entirely." I took that to heart, and now I feel free to be selective and only read the parts that I find helpful and engaging in certain books. Rob's advice was freeing. I "feed" on certain books only until I am satisfied.

Third, **whatever we do with our reading; let's not hurry it.** The primary pace of comprehension that we desire in the establishment of the soul's reading room requires that we slow down. There is a legitimate place for speed reading of some books, but the recommended tempo, especially

---

43. Stephen Um, *1 Corinthians: The Word of the Cross* (Wheaton, IL: Crossway, 2015), 44-45.

for Christian devotional classics that have passed the test of time, demands that they not be read hurriedly. They must be tasted slowly. They must be eaten reflectively. The chief aim of this kind of reading is to deepen our house's footings so that more and more, we resemble the King we love. We want to become better listeners to Jesus, who can speak to us through these great classics. There are contemporary authors whose works can be read and comprehended sufficiently in far less time. But if we are going to read the dead guys, we should not read them at a fast pace. Certain authors of the past often require a slower pace. I applaud and embrace the helpful questions David McKenna raised in *How to Read a Christian Book.* He asks: "Is this book true to the inspired Word of God? Is this book useful for Christian teaching? Does this book contribute to Christian maturity?"[44] These questions remind me that the kind of reading I want to do cannot be hurried.

Fourth, **we should practice gathering our reading around a single theme or author.** This application is important in the establishment of a reading room that can last a lifetime. John Wesley is reported to have said, "Read or get out of the ministry." Those are blunt words, but wise ones. One of the voices that has greatly impacted my life is that of Eugene Peterson. For a season, I grouped several of his books together and simply read him regularly and often. In one of Eugene's lesser-known books, *Take and Read. Spiritual Reading: An Annotated List,* he observed that many of us have impulses from time to time to live a holy life. Then someone telephones, dinner needs to be prepared, or the lawn requires mowing, and we find ourselves distracted by the mundane. In response, Peterson offered this insightful council. He wrote:

> "And then we find ourselves in the company of a writer or writers who penetrate the surface pieties and show us what the holy life is like... All Christians, in some way or another, are about

---

44. David McKenna, *How to Read a Christian Book* (Grand Rapids, MI: Baker, 2001), 47-54.

the business of holy living… Herman Melville once wrote to a friend, 'I love all men who dive.' Most of us do. But where do we find them? Not in the men and women who attract attention. The trivial and evil feed the appetite for gossip in a journalistic culture. Neither goodness nor righteousness makes headlines. Anything that cannot be programmed for mass production, particularly moral excellence, is discarded. Maturity, since it cannot be mastered in a semester course, in no longer a personal goal. Our ancestors were wiser. They looked around for saints, looked for the men and women whose lives were courageously conversant with God, and let them be their teachers in how to live as human beings, which is to say, how to live holy lives."[45]

A helpful method is to group significant voices. Read all that A.W. Tozer wrote. Digest C.S. Lewis' many books. Devour John R.W. Stott. Take the time to discover all that Philip Yancey has written on the subject of pain. Sit down and learn from Annie Dillard, Virginia Stem Owens, Flannery O'Connor and other women who have written extensively and deeply.

Fifth, **we should meditate, pray and journal over what we read.** I believe in capturing what I read. I do that through writing things down. I like to weigh and consider what I am reading. Sometimes I try to memorize a line or two from the good books that I am reading. When I first read Francis Bacon, I was struck by his statement: "Read not to contradict and confute, nor to believe and take for granted, nor to find talk and discourse, but read to weigh." He believed that some books are to be tasted, others swallowed, and some few books are to be chewed entirely and digested. I like that. Give that some thought. You may have the capacity to take notes and jot things down digitally on your tablet, iPad, or other device. I am an old guy, and I like the texture of paper and the feel of a leather journal. The method matters little, but we need to find a place of storage so that what we read is retrievable and

---

[45]. Eugene Peterson, *Take and Read. Spiritual Reading: An Annotated List* (Grand Rapids, MI: Eerdmans, 1996), 92-93.

we can harvest the notes we take.

Sixth, as previous points have demonstrated, **we should learn to ask the right questions as we read.** In the back of Karen Swallow Prior's superb book, *On Reading Well: Finding the Good Life through Great Books*, this author offers helpful questions around her central reading themes of prudence, temperance, justice, courage, faith, hope, love, chastity, diligence, patience, kindness and humility. Her questions are excellent. Authors Jamin Goggin and Kyle Strobel, in an exceptionally helpful book, remind all of us that the fundamental goals of reading spiritual classics include these: loving God and neighbor, being mature in Christ, training in righteousness and ultimately bringing glory to God. Does my reading include those ultimate ends?[46] David McKenna offers exceptionally helpful advice as we examine our reading habits. He suggests that we imagine ourselves exiled on an isolated island and find ourselves able to take only our Bible and ten other books. He raises these good questions:

> "What books would make up your library in exile? What classic Christian books do you want to read and reread? As you begin to read books that will lead to your own Christian understanding and spiritual growth, you will make discoveries that you can claim as your own. Like an explorer mapping the way over uncharted territory, you will find classic books that serve as landmarks showing the way and contemporary books that serve as locators defining reality… God's Word and the book that are commentaries on his Word will still be communicators of the faith 'once delivered to the saints.'"[47]

Seventh, **we should constantly sharpen our reading tools.** The same principles that applied to our Word-intake are the same ones that will sharpen our reading of other books. First, make reading a priority. Select the best

---

46. Jamin Goggin and Kyle Strobel, *Reading the Christian Spiritual Classics* (Downers Grove, IL: IVP, 2013), 35.
47. McKenna, *How to Read a Christian Book*, 121.

books. Make the time and take the time to set up a reading list. Do whatever it takes to get your hands on the best books. Ask, buy, borrow, beg. This kind of zeal for reading always makes me think of Paul. I hear Paul's plea for books in that dank, terrible, dark, depressing Mamertine Prison. He wrote to Timothy: "When you come, bring the cloak that I left with Carpus at Troas, also the books, and above all the parchments" (2 Timothy 4:13). There is a lot of debate over what Paul meant by books and parchments and each one of us may sort that out, but I like the plainness of John Stott's analysis of books and parchments. Stott wrote:

> "The difference between the two is probably that the former were made of papyrus rather than parchment. These papyrus rolls may have been writing materials or his correspondence or some official documents, even perhaps his certificate of Roman citizenship. The parchments may conceivably have been unused (NEB, 'my notebooks'). But it seems more probable that they were 'books' of some kind, and the most likely guess is 'Paul's version of the Old Testament in Greek, no small burden to carry around,' and/or 'possibly official copies of the Lord's words or early narratives of his life'… Of course some Christians today scorn reading and study altogether, and assert that they would not feel the need of books at any time, let alone in prison… But we should note that this passage commends continual reading to all godly (people) as a thing from which they can profit."[48]

Paul's request exemplifies the value of reading for his soul's sake and is a strong reminder of the legitimate place of reading in our soul's care and maintenance. Paul was held in the Mamertine Prison, a hellhole that was devoted primarily to political prisoners and is the oldest prison in the Western world. If you visit that infamous prison now, winding steel steps lead into a hole that smells of urine and worse. As I visited this ancient

---

48. John Stott, *The Message of 2 Timothy: Guard the Gospel. The Bible Speaks Today* (Downers Grove, IL: IVP, 1973), 120-121.

dungeon, I was gripped by its darkness, confinement, smell, and the chains that held Paul to solid rock walls. The reality of what this saint experienced overwhelmed me completely. I cannot imagine how Paul endured it. Even as I was repulsed, I told my wife that I needed to remain there alone for a few minutes to feel what Paul had so unflinchingly endured. I made it only a few seconds before I began to sob. I was reminded in that dark and lonely place, Paul said, "Timothy, bring me my books and don't forget my coat. It is cold down here." Paul knew the priority of reading.

Second, find a favorite place where you settle in to read. Make that place a comfortable and quiet spot. My longtime friend, Judy Parmenter, has such a place in her house. She has a little rocking chair with a lamp and a small bookshelf where she keeps her Bible, a book that she is currently reading, her journal and some of her Bible study resources. She has made a place suitable for her own soul care.

Third, we must persevere. We must stick to our reading. I have always admired Eugene Peterson's example of finding a rhythm for his own reading life. He regularly made time on Tuesday and Thursday afternoons for reading. I could never quite find that much space in my schedule, so I decided to be faithful to carving out a minimum of 15 minutes a day beyond Scripture-intake to read. Think of the enormous benefit it would make to our life, over several decades, if we could find some small bit of time every day to read. Note the difference between what Gordon McDonald used to call "offensive reading vs. defensive reading." Defensive reading is what we read just to survive. Offensive reading is going beyond what is required, and reading authors and books that deepen us, grow us and help us serve others better. Persevere in a daily commitment to reading.

Finally, always keep a pen and some paper nearby. If you prefer digital note taking, keep that tablet, iPhone or iPad close. You may even choose to write in your books. Many of my books are filled with notes. Mark, circle, underline and take notes voraciously.

I once experienced a dreaded state of depression (melancholy). Fierce criticism, actually a tsunami of criticism was aimed at me, and I had not managed my margins well. I was exhausted and my heart was broken. The attacks had leveled my soul. On Sunday evening, after consulting with a dear and trusted elder in the church, Sue took our hamper full of dirty clothes and tossed it into the trunk of our car. It served as our luggage. We put the kids into their pajamas, loaded up whatever toiletries and snacks we thought we might need, and drove all night. We ended up in Arkansas where my wife's parents lived. I have never been the kind of person who sleeps in, but once we arrived at their home, I got in bed and stayed in bed. I was clearly in an unhealthy state.

My mother-in-law, Velores Graham, (1930-2021) was my book finder for decades. Her recent death has left an immense void in our family. She kept my ongoing book list so that she could go to estate sales and library giveaways and try to find the authors and books I wanted. When we arrived as refugees in the dark, and she saw me languishing, she discerned my unhealthy soul, drove to the local library sale and found the just-right book for me, *The Life of David Livingstone,* by J.H. Worcester. You may recall that Livingstone was the great African missionary and explorer. As she returned from her book search, my mother-in-law stopped at the grocery store and bought me a king size Snickers candy bar. (I ate sugar in those days.) She knocked firmly on the bedroom door and said, "Here, enjoy. Don't come out until you are done." She tossed me the Snickers bar and book. I devoured that Snickers bar and reluctantly started reading Livingstone's biography. I did not get out of bed until I finished that biography the next day. I concluded that if Livingstone could endure all the challenges and heartaches that he did, I could as well. After two weeks of rest, we drove back home and ultimately experienced the most fruitful years of that ministry. The right book at the right moment helped restore my soul's house. May it be so with you as well.

CHAPTER 8

WHAT IF MY SOUL'S HOUSE HAS NO READING ROOM?

> *"Some souls, like some people, can be slummy anywhere… Others can achieve in the most impossible situation a simple and beautiful life. The good citizen must be able without reluctance to open the door at all times, not only at the week-end; must keep the windows clean and taps running properly, that the light and living water may come in."*[49]

Evelyn understood that the maintenance of our soul's house matters. The just right reading plays a significant role in that ongoing upkeep. What should I do if reading books is not my passion? What if I discover in the near future that I am just weary of study? What if I am simply tired of exploring someone else's thoughts and writings? What if the people with whom I am ministering do not value reading as a holy habit? What do I do then? If we are honest, some of us try to be readers and discover that we are not really readers at all. We do our best and muddle our way through the reading of

---

49. Underhill, *Concerning the Inner Life*, 72-73.

books. At some point, the enemy of our souls leverages guilt and manipulates us into believing that the reading of many books is a non-negotiable in the care of our soul. We believe we are deficient in the Jesus-following journey because we lack a hearty appetite for ongoing reading. There is grace in this holy habit. Rest in the truth that there are different kinds of reading. What can we read, other than a book, that might help us to accomplish the same objective in nurturing our soul's house?

First, **we can read creation.** We can encourage other people to read creation. One of my heroes of faith, Charles Spurgeon, the great British preacher of the nineteenth century, learned to read creation well. He wrote:

> "Can you not learn from nature? Every flower is waiting to teach you. 'Consider the lilies,' and learn from the roses. Not only may you go to the ant, but every living thing offers itself for your instruction. There is a voice in every gale, a lesson in every grain of dust it bears. Sermons glisten in the morning on every blade of grass, and homilies fly by you as the leaves fall from the trees. A forest is a library; a cornfield is a volume of philosophy, the rock is a history, and the river at its base a poem. Come thou who has thine eyes opened, and find lessons of wisdom everywhere, in heaven above, in the earth beneath and in the waters under the earth. Books are poor things compared with these."[50]

Read what God has created. Although creation cannot reveal the specifics of the Jesus-following life, it reveals a wealth of insight about our Triune God. Paul didn't want us to miss this. He said: "For his invisible attributes, namely, his eternal power and divine nature, have been clearly perceived, ever since the creation of the world, in the things that have been made" (Romans 1:20).

I pray that you have experienced what Paul described, and find that creation speaks to your soul. Perhaps like me, you have made reflection on

---

50. C.H. Spurgeon, *Spurgeon's Lectures to His Students*, condensed and abridged by David Otis Fuller (Grand Rapids, MI: Zondervan, 1945), 166.

creation into a holy habit that you practice routinely. Your appreciation of God's creation is far more important than your geographic location. You may love a state park nearby, or simply walk near your home. My walks near Kickapoo Creek remind me of Mary Francis and Dan Harper, two people the Lord provided as surrogate parents for me. They loved me well during a time in my life when I was falling into a dark abyss of sin and rebellion. Their evening walks with their dogs modeled the holy habit of a sweet time of enjoying each other's company and reflecting and praying together. I am sure they bathed those walks in prayer for their three children, their work, their lives together and their concern for me. We need to periodically ask our own soul some questions. How have I experienced creation recently? Have I intentionally taken the time to "read" what God has made and listen to what it might teach me about His character? What does my current reading of creation look like? I am a better person when I take the time to read what God has made. My wife would agree.

Second, **we can read our own heart.** I think of Jeremiah when I consider this form of reading. Jeremiah said: "The heart is deceitful above all things, and desperately sick; who can understand it" (Jeremiah 17:9)? I believe the most difficult and challenging book that any of us will ever read is our own heart. This can be painful, but it is important to take the time and space to do this. So many before us have recognized the value of self-examination. Ignatius of Loyola, John Wesley, and even contemporary authors like Peter Scazzero have recognized the importance of reading our own heart. A simple prayer of asking God why my heart is troubled is sufficient. I inquire: "Father, why am I reacting the way I am reacting? Help me understand myself. I don't like what I am seeing in me." Again, I turn to the wise words of Spurgeon. He wrote:

> "Study yourself. This is a mysterious volume, the major part of which you have not read… Watch the twists and turns and

singularities of your own mind, and the strangeness of your own experience; the depravity of your heart, and the work of divine grace; your tendency to sin, and your capacity for holiness; how akin you are to a devil, and yet how allied to God Himself! Note how wisely you can act when taught of God, and how foolishly you behave when left to yourself. You will find the study of your heart to be of immense importance to you as a watcher over the souls of others."[51]

Not long ago, I read through the Psalms again. I circled all the occasions that the word "soul" occurred. I counted ninety-seven occurrences. My goal was to notice what the various contributors to the Psalter said about their own souls, what they said to their souls, and how they were asking God to help them understand what was going on in their interior world. I was particularly drawn to Psalms 42 and 43. In those twin Psalms, there is a refrain shaped as a question. The Psalmist asked: "Why are you cast down, O my soul, and why are you in turmoil within me? Hope in God; for I shall again praise him, my salvation and my God" (42:5, 11 and 43:5). Clearly, the writer had taken the time to read his own heart. That brief study gave me the permission and grace to read my own soul's house carefully and intentionally.

Third, **we can read other people.** Spurgeon said: "Read other men. They are as instructive as books."[52] Of course, we need to be considerate with this suggestion and this different way of "reading." Sometimes when Sue is shopping, I find a quiet spot and read for a while. Then I pause my reading and turn to people reading. I wonder about those I see. Do they know Jesus? Are they in pain? Are they sad, mad, glad or worried? Where is their joy found? Are they lonely? My people reading sometimes causes me to stop, pray and intercede for them. Sometimes, I experience intense joy when I see the love parents have for their children or see people showing kindness to

---

51. Spurgeon, *Spurgeon's Lectures*, 167.
52. Ibid., 168.

one another. Other times, my people reading saddens me when I see people arguing and shouting. As you read others, remember that only God knows and sees the heart (1 Samuel 16:7, Psalm 44:21, Jeremiah 17:10 and Romans 8:27). Reading other people is a legitimate way of practicing the discipline of reading, but we must prepare by reading our own hearts first.

Fourth, **we can read thin places**. The term "thin places" is what the Celts called those places where the distance between heaven and earth collapsed. They describe moments in time where God pulled back the curtain and allowed those Celtic Christians to see what they otherwise would miss. Although not so named, the whole notion of thin places pre-existed the Christian Celts. Although Scripture does not use this metaphor, I think of places like Mt. Sinai, the tent of meeting, and the burning bush as potential examples of what the Celts experienced. Moses encountered God deeply and intimately at Sinai, the tent of meeting and the burning bush. From my study, the Celtic Christians thought of mysterious and mesmerizing places like the windy island of Iona (now part of Scotland) or the majestic and rocky peaks of Croagh Patrick as thin places.

The Celts believed heaven and earth were only three feet apart, but in thin places that distance became even shorter. Weddings and funerals are often thin spaces. It is so necessary to pay attention to what makes us joyful, what makes us laugh or cry. Sometimes, in offering spiritual direction, I will ask: When was the last time you experienced a belly laugh? What had happened and why did it bring you such joy? When was the last time you had a good cry? Do you believe that everyone needs a good cry periodically? What caused your tears to flow? I want people who walk with Jesus to notice how God is present in times of great joy and times of great sadness. Our ancient Celtic Christian brothers and sisters, St. Patrick among them, experienced thin places in groves of trees, at waterfalls, near ponds, rivers, and on the ocean itself. They believed that such places made your own importance shrink, and magnified the greatness of God and His creation. Those who worship the creation rather than the Creator, and see only what is in front of them, never reach the thin places. But what I have noticed is when I take the time to notice and think about thin places, I have an opportunity to do a unique kind of reading.

There was a pre-COVID period when I was traveling a great deal and I would arrive at the airport early. The airport sounds like a strange location for a thin place, but I would find a quiet spot. I would drink my coffee, read my Bible, and simply ponder what I read, saw, heard and experienced. God would often speak into that airport time in ways that refreshed me.

Fifth, **we can read books indirectly by simply listening to them.** Sue, my beloved wife, has been listening to the entire audio Harry Potter series as she commutes to work. She and I have discussed the spiritual value of this series and how, as a professor, I view this reading, and the value of audio books. I believe the metaphors of good versus evil are well worth contemplating. We cannot ignore the dangers of dark magic and evil represented, but as believers, such battle stories can stimulate our imaginations and make us more God-aware. We read everything through the lens of Gospel truth and take every thought captive to Christ. Audio recordings are another way to "read." We can also read through watching movies.

For my servant leadership side, I annually re-watch Daniel Day Lewis' portrait of President Lincoln. Witnessing Lincoln's sacrificial life and especially his ability to grieve every Thursday in a small room he designated in the White House has energized me and encouraged me to face my own grief. Lincoln would grieve over the loss of his children. He would grieve over the great break between the North and the South. He allowed himself to grieve over the slavery issue. I believe that because Lincoln lamented weekly, he did not lose hope.

Wise Charles Spurgeon reminds all of us: "Without books a person may learn much by keeping his eyes open. Current history, incidents which transpire under his own nose, events recorded in the newspaper, matters of common talk—he may learn from them all."[53] Karl Barth, a Swiss theologian of the twentieth century, encouraged us to read with the Bible in one hand and the newspaper in the other hand. Reading everything that affects our everyday life is a good and healthy practice, as long as we see it all and consider it all through the life of our Savior and Redeemer. Again, I repeat what the great Spurgeon said: "If you have no books to try your eyes, keep them open wherever you go and you will find something worth looking at. Can you not learn from nature? Every flower is waiting to teach you."[54]

So, how do I live, read and think as an apprentice of Jesus and as a builder of the soul's house? There are two really important principles that I want to make perfectly clear. All of us, without exception, tend to be busy and driven. We make little room for reading. If we are not careful, we get sucked into the muck and mire of shallow living. Yet when we are alone, pouring our hearts out to the Father, we recognize our longing for that ordered inner home that gives our King a place to live, speak, enjoy, rule and reign. Those two realities—hurry and hunger—battle each other daily. Reading can be a rest stop, a gift that regulates our speed and slows us down to see and hear the voice of the One who loves us. Evelyn Underhill understood the essential nature of keeping the soul's house in good condition.

---

53. Spurgeon, *Spurgeon's Lectures*, 166-167.
54. Ibid., 167.

CHAPTER 9

A ROOM FOR EATING, DIGESTING AND RUMINATING ON THE WORD

> *"We can afford to have a warm and well-furnished kitchen, and even to take pride in it, so long as we remember that it is a kitchen; and that all its activities must be subservient to the interests of the whole house, and its observance of the city's law."*[55]

The soul's house, according to Evelyn, needs a room for eating, digesting and ruminating on God's Word. This is the soul's kitchen or dining room; a room for a spiritual practice called Christian meditation. What the comma is to grammar, Christian meditation is to the Jesus follower. A comma is a pause. It is not a period. It is not a place to stop. Meditation is a slowing down, a yielding of an hour or so to ponder what you have gleaned from Scripture. Just as the kitchen or dining room is a place to prepare food and enjoy the pleasure of eating it, so there needs to be a place where we pause during the day and dine on the Scriptures. I appreciate the way Donald Whitney

---

55. Underhill, *Concerning the Inner Life*, 86.

describes this wise and necessary practice. Whitney writes:

> "One sad feature of our modern culture is that meditation has become identified more with non-Christian systems of thought than with biblical Christianity. Even among believers, the practice of meditation is often more closely associated with yoga, transcendental meditation, relaxation therapy, or the New Age Movement. Because meditation is so prominent in many spiritually counterfeit groups and movements, some Christians are uncomfortable with the whole subject and suspicious of those who engage in it. But we must remember that meditation is both commanded by God and modeled by the godly in Scripture. Just because a cult uses the cross as a symbol doesn't mean the Church should cease to use it. In the same way, we shouldn't discard or be afraid of scriptural meditation simply because the world has adapted it for its own purposes… Let's define meditation as deep thinking on the truths and spiritual realities revealed in Scripture for the purposes of understanding, application, and prayer."[56]

If you have had the opportunity to read Richard Foster's *Celebration of Discipline,* you already know the simple way he defines this holy habit. Foster says:

> "Christian meditation… is the ability to hear God's voice and obey his word… What happens in meditation is that we create the emotional and spiritual space which allows Christ to construct an inner sanctuary in the heart… It is a portable sanctuary that is brought into all we are and do."[57]

Meditation always reminds me of the *Selah* notations in the Psalms. It is clear that the various contributors to the Psalter thought there was a legitimate place for an occasional interlude. There is considerable debate

---

56. Whitney, *Spiritual Disciplines for the Christian Life*, 43-44.
57. Richard Foster, *Celebration of Discipline: The Path of Spiritual Growth*, 25th Anniversary (New York, NY: Harper-Collins, 1998), 17, 20.

among scholars about what purpose these pauses serve, but it seems that they are placed strategically in 39 of the Psalms to indicate some kind of brief musical interlude or a short liturgical response. *Selah* markers invite a pause. In just that way, the Christian life needs commas and pauses.

There are two significant Hebrew words for meditation in the Old Testament Bible. The first, and the one that I most gravitate toward is "*hagah*" or "*hawgah*." It is the most common Hebrew word for meditation. A wonderful example is Psalm 1. The psalmist said of the righteous man: "His delight is in the law of the LORD and in his law, he meditates day and night" (Psalm 1:2). "*Hagah*" literally means to murmur to yourself or to make a low sound; what we would call muttering or talking to ourselves. Such an activity may sound strange to our twenty-first century ears and minds but it is appropriately descriptive. Hebrew poetry also uses this word *hagah* to describe the cooing sound of a dove, the growling of a lion when he has captured his meal for the day, or even the sound a mourner makes during a season of grief. This is the sound of the deep satisfaction or concentration that we experience during meditation.

Eugene Peterson was right when he suggested that the best way to think of meditation, at least from a Hebrew point of view, was to think about a dog with a bone. Peterson wrote:

> "In the language of the psalmist, this word meditate has to do with slow eating… I thought of a dog I once owned. When we were on summer vacations in Montana, he loved to explore the foothills where we stayed. He often came across the carcass of a white-tailed deer brought down by coyotes. Later he would show up on our lakeside patio dragging a shank or a rib. He was a small dog, and the bone was often nearly as large as he was. Anyone who has owned a dog knows the routine: he would prance and gambol playful before us with his prize, wagging his tail, proud of his find, courting our approval. And of course, we approved: we

lavished praise, telling him what a good dog he was… He would drag the bone twenty yards or so to a more private place… He gnawed the bone, turned it over, licked it, worried it. Sometimes we would hear a low rumble or growl. He was obviously enjoying himself and was in no hurry. For a leisurely couple of hours, he would enjoy the bone, then bury it, and return the next day to take it up again… My dog meditated his bone. You and I meditate the revelation in Scripture and Jesus."[58]

A bone, like the one Peterson described above, cannot be devoured. It must be savored. Gnawing is required. Christian meditation is like that. It is the process of slowly savoring God's Word, ruminating on what we discover and taking it into our inner world. We chew on the thoughts of God, we think about Him and what He has said in Christ. Christian meditation is whispering to ourselves about Him, His nature, His purpose, His plan, His character, and His Son.

The second Hebrew word for meditation is "*suach*" or "*siah*." It is used several times in Psalm 119. One example will do. Psalm 119:15 says: "I will meditate on your precepts and fix my eyes on your ways." In that verse and other surrounding verses, "The basic meaning of this verb seems to be 'rehearse,' or 'go over a matter in one's mind.'"[59] The New Testament word that most resembles this Old Testament word for meditating is "*meletao*," the word for diligently pondering something (1 Timothy 4:15).

There is a Latin term that might offer some help in our understanding of Christian meditation. I claim no expertise with Latin, but I like this specific word, because it paints a picture of meditation in creation. The word is "*florilegia*" which literally means "flower sipping." Imagine a bee drawing nectar while moving from flower to flower. This very activity occurs in my

---

58. Eugene Peterson, *As Kingfishers Catch Fire* (Colorado Springs, CO: WaterBrook, 2017), 108-109.
59. R.L. Harris, G.L. Archer and B.K. Waltke, *Theological Wordbook of the Old Testament. Volume 2* (Chicago, IL: Moody Press, 1980), 875.

own backyard when bees and hummingbirds draw nectar from my wife's flowers. Bees and hummingbirds help us grasp the meaning of Christian meditation. Even the ancient monks and nuns provide a worthy portrait of spiritual flower sipping. For them, this meant memorizing short Bible passages and the sayings of the early Church Fathers while drawing the nectar out of what they memorized. They meditated upon those thoughts as they worked through the day. The *Florilegia* for the soul is not just for bees, hummingbirds and monastics.

Hagah, suach, and *florilegia,* and other words like them, help us understand the nature and purpose of eating, digesting and ruminating on God's Word. Years ago, Elton Trueblood, the great Quaker thinker and teacher used a metaphor that reminds me of the urgency of Christian meditation. Trueblood called the North American landscape a "cut flower civilization." By that, he meant that we were a people without deep roots. Because I love my wife, I sometimes buy her a bouquet of flowers. She has a knack for keeping them beautiful and alive by recutting the stems and adding floral food to the water. Even with all that Sue does, the flowers wilt and die. Like those flowers, we are a culture without deep roots. What Christian meditation can do is help us become people with vibrant and healthy roots in Christ. I believe that meditation is the antidote to shallowness in our Christian lives.

What prevents so many of us from practicing this discipline? Donald Whitney's observation above offers plenty of potential answers. Meditation's association with yoga, transcendental meditation, relaxation therapy, or the New Age Movement has affected us. Even our schedules and uneasiness with silence keep us from Christian meditation.

So how do we begin to incorporate this holy habit into our everyday life and into our soul's house? Here are three practical suggestions. First, **we can learn the basic principle of rumination.** Cattle can teach us a thing or two about Christian meditation. Cows are created with multiple stomach compartments. What they graze on in the morning moves back up into their mouths to be chewed again: the "cud." They appear to enjoy this re-chewing and do it daily. We can take a lesson from the lowly cow by taking in God's Word in the morning, pondering it, chewing on it and then bringing it back up to chew on again during the day. This isn't the prettiest metaphor, but it's helpful.

Second, **we can implement the principle of selection**. I have many Jesus-following friends who have decided to be very discriminating about what they spend their time thinking about throughout the day. They choose a verse from Scripture each morning, planting it in their heart and meditating on it repeatedly throughout the day. All of us can do that. Tim Keller describes this practice so well. He writes:

> "Meditation is spiritually 'tasting' the Scripture—delighting in it, sensing the sweetness of the teaching, feeling the conviction of what it tells us about ourselves, and thanking God and praising God for what it shows us about him. Meditation is also spiritually 'digesting' the Scripture–applying it, thinking out how it affects you, describes you, guides you in the most practical way. It is drawing strength from the Scripture, letting it give you hope, using it to remember how loved you are. To shift metaphors, meditation is taking the truth down into our hearts until it catches fire there and begins to melt and shape our reactions to God, ourselves, and the world."[60]

Third, **we can apply the principle of imagination**. We Jesus followers require an exercised imagination. We must always be looking for the grace of God at work in our everyday lives. As children, we have abundant imagination, but it seems our imaginations wane as we become adults. Maybe the following will help explain this principle:

When I was a child, there were three places of safety I would run to

---
60. Keller, *Prayer,* 150-151.

when things exploded in my home. First, there was Kickapoo Creek where I built myself a shaky treehouse. It would have failed any building code, but it was mine and it was my escape. I would run that well-worn path between the parsonage, the nearby grain bins and the tributary that ran into Kickapoo Creek. In that treehouse, things would somehow get sorted out in my troubled heart. For hours, I would hide there, out of my father's line of fire. I would imagine that I had a shelf full of my favorite foods, a pocket full of money, and a heart full of peace. My imagination would create a fortress where I was protected.

A second place I would go, when I could, was a Christian camp called Little Galilee which was twenty minutes from my house in Clinton, Illinois. Even though I wasn't yet a Christ-follower, I found hope and serenity there as people talked about Jesus. I loved listening to the singing and the devotional reflections around the campfire. Little Galilee was one of those thin places where God seemed to break through the world of my troubled childhood. There, I imagined that my life somehow made sense and that there was a spot for me, somewhere, that was full of purpose and joy.

A third place of safety was my grandmother's farm. I was sixteen when my grandfather died in 1969, but Grandma remained on the farm without him. She was incredibly tough and tender. Her toughness enabled her to stay on that farm alone for another twenty plus years and she died in her rocking chair looking out over the land she loved. With her Bible in her lap, she rocked herself into heaven. Grandma's tender side was evident in her attentiveness to me, and to all her grandchildren. She had only a sixth-grade education, but she earned a PhD in life experience. Grandma loved the Lord with all her heart, and was faithful to her daily time of reading and reflecting on the Word. When I asked her why she read her Bible every morning, her reply was filled with Proverb-like wisdom. She said, "I am a leaky bucket. I need refilled every day." When Kenneth Taylor published his *Living Bible*, my grandmother bought a copy. She told me she could not understand the *King James Version* and that Taylor's plain language made sense to her. Grandma and I had conversations as we sipped sweet tea on her west-facing cement patio and watched the sun set. Her common life inspired me to live an uncommon life. She held tutorials there at sunset on the priority of Christian imagination and I was her pupil. Grandma's holy habit of reading Scripture in the morning and then meditating on it while gathering eggs from the chicken coop, butchering chickens in the barnyard, slopping the hogs with leftover meal scraps, or tending to her large garden filled my imagination with the possibility of keeping company with God. She chewed on God's Word in every nook and cranny of that farm and I was the beneficiary. My imagination was set on fire by a humble woman with a grade-school education. She made me believe that there was not a single part of our existence through which God could not speak.

Finally, remind yourself that meditation is the minute-by-minute practice of keeping the Word of the Lord at the forefront of our thoughts. We cannot do this without holy inspiration, so ask the Holy Spirit to refresh you through eating, digesting and ruminating on the Scriptures. Your soul's dining room is waiting.

CHAPTER 10

THE SOUL'S HOUSE AND THE NEEDED SECURITY SYSTEM

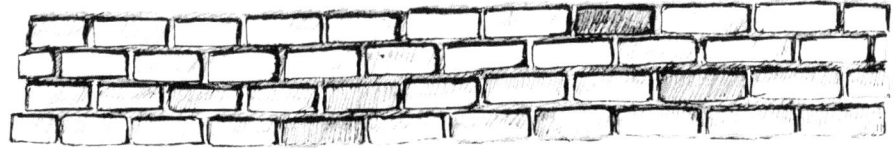

> *"Temperance, then, must preside over the furnishing of the soul's house, if it is to be the setting of a useful, ordered, peaceful interior life… The spiritual life of man is never without an element of conflict."*[61]

The market for home security systems is soaring. Protection experts list many benefits of investing in their product. Such systems offer peace of mind, reduced insurance premiums, and are a deterrent to burglars. These troubling times may induce you to buy a security system for your home, but my concerns about security go far beyond brick and mortar. Far more needed is the necessary soul protection required to be fully alert to the spiritual war that surrounds us, to fight the good fight, and to finish well. Our enemy, who is not of flesh and blood, seeks to burglarize and destroy our interior world. Jesus followers committed to cooperating with the Holy Spirit and seeking Christlikeness are in for the fight of their lives. Does my soul's house have a good security system?

---

61. Underhill, *Concerning the Inner Life*, 87 and 101.

For a time professionally, I had one foot in the classroom at Lincoln Christian University and one foot at the Jefferson Street Christian Church in Lincoln, Illinois. Dr. Robert Lowery (1948-2011), a distinguished New Testament seminary professor at Lincoln Christian University, was a faithful member at Jeff Street and a true servant there. I have always enjoyed team teaching, and as a professor and pastor, I took the opportunity to have Bob join me in teaching and preaching at our annual Christmas Eve worship service. We decided to team teach and preach about the first Bethlehem audience, about those first eyewitnesses of the incarnation: angels, shepherds, Mary and Joseph.

The Lincoln Fire Marshal was also a member at Jeff St. and was never happy about all the seating we had to add to accommodate all those who flocked to the Christmas Eve service, but we never wanted to turn anyone away. People loved being part of that special worship service of music and decorations. I encouraged Bob to join me in bringing out our absolute best teaching that night. We decorated a front table with large Willow Tree Nativity figurines. We had oxen, goats, lambs, cattle, donkeys, camels, angels, shepherds, Mary, Joseph, baby Jesus and even wise men who remained just outside of the manger scene to remind us that they arrived sometime later. Bob insisted that we were still missing a vital piece to that Advent story. Based on Revelation 12, we needed to add the great red dragon! I have no idea where Bob found it, but he brought a great red dragon with seven heads, ten horns and seven diadems (Revelation 12:3) and spoke eloquently of an enemy who was out to demolish, devour and destroy. The children were awed and the grownups were stunned.

Not many of us have thought about an Advent war arising in heaven between Michael and his angels on one side and the great red dragon and his angels on the other side. John, the writer of Revelation, described the scene this way: "And the dragon stood before the woman who was about to give birth, so that when she bore her child he might devour it. She gave birth to a male child, one who is to rule all the nations with a rod of iron, but her child was caught up to God and to his throne" (Revelation 12:4-5). Even the incarnation is a reminder of a colossal spiritual war.

There are four primary spiritual warfare principles that enable us to establish a good security system over our soul's house. **The first principle is to simply recognize that we are at war.** The apostle Peter knew this well. He said, "Be sober-minded; be watchful. Your adversary the devil prowls around like a roaring lion, seeking someone to devour. Resist him" (1 Peter 5:8-9a). This universal war began is alluded to in places like Isaiah 41:12-15, and Ezekiel 28:15-19. Genesis 3:1-19 and is our reminder that the enemy is at work to destroy all the good that God had created. I appreciate the plain manner in which Ken Boa describes the nature and work of our enemy, Satan. He writes:

> "Both the Old and New Testaments repeatedly acknowledge the existence of Satan. Scripture teaches that he is a personal being who possesses intellect, emotion, and will (Zechariah 3:1-2; Luke 4:1-13; 2 Corinthians 11:3; Revelation 20:7-8). He was created by God as an angel (Isaiah 14:12-13; Matthew 25:41; Revelation 12:9), and as 'the anointed cherub,' he was originally perfect in beauty and blameless in his ways until his rebellion against God (Ezekiel 28:12-15). He is evidently the most powerful creature God ever made (Jude 9). His heart was lifted up because of his beauty; his splendor corrupted his wisdom, and he raised himself up against God in an act of titanic self-assertion (Ezekiel 28:16-17; Isaiah 14:12-15; these prophetic passages refer to historical characters, but it appears that the poetry also uses these figures to allude to a cosmic dimension of spiritual evil). Because of his rebellion, Satan's character was distorted, and he became a powerful force of evil in the universe."[62]

---

62. Ken Boa, *Conformed to His Image* (Grand Rapids, MI: Zondervan, 2001), 340-341.

The devil is described as a slanderer, destroyer, tempter, accuser, deceiver, murderer and liar. As ruler of this world (John 12:31; 16:11), he leads an ongoing war against our Triune God. Anyone foolish enough to think he can battle Satan on his own is as unprepared as the soldier who enters a battle without training, armor and weapons. Because of Christ's victory at the cross over sin, death and the devil, we do not have to be fearful or fascinated by the enemy of our soul. Instead, we "put on the whole armor of God, that we may be able to stand against the schemes of the devil" (Ephesians 6:11). As paradoxical as it sounds, we have already won the war, but the battle continues.

There is a second spiritual warfare principle that can help us secure our soul's house. **The second spiritual warfare principle is that this war is being fought on at least three primary fronts.** These fronts include the heavens, the mind and the church. Not everyone agrees on these three fronts, but I offer these for your consideration. Ephesians 6:12 is our reminder of the titanic conflict taking place in the heavens; the realms we cannot see. 2 Corinthians 4:4 is our reminder that the enemy has targeted and blinded the minds of unbelievers. The battle assignment of every Jesus follower is to "take every thought captive to obey Christ" (2 Corinthians 10:5). Revelation 2 and 3 is our reminder that Satan attacks the church through cunning strategies. For those who would argue that the home is a primary battle front, we do not disagree because I have always believed that the home is the first church.

There is controversy about this third front, the church. My point is simple; the devil has already won the world. His pervasive influence is everywhere on the planet. But above all else, he specifically wants to crush the Bride of Christ. Be comforted by the words of Jesus about the church: "The gates of hell shall not prevail against it" (Matthew 16:18). The enemy used all kinds of tactics to destroy the early church in Corinth: division, quarreling, lawsuits, sexual immorality, disagreements over food offered to idols and many others. Paul's letters in the New Testament clearly reveal spiritual warfare among the churches that probably kept him up at night. If you've noted and grieved over divisions in church congregations, you know that the church is one of the major battle fronts of the enemy.

For a short time, I was a youth pastor of a small central Illinois congregation. I know now that I was not suited for youth ministry, but I worked at it for two years. I had no business being a youth pastor, but I wanted to serve, and it was a good place to take my first steps in ministry. Because of squabbles in the church between the preacher and some of the members, there were Saturday nights when the preacher would say, "I am going to be gone tomorrow and I need you to preach." I loved that church so I would stay up all night and prepare a sermon for Sunday morning.

I remember a specific youth Sunday, where the kids took the primary role of leading the worship service. After teaching the high school class, I headed upstairs, and encountered an argument between one of the church elders and the preacher's wife. It was ugly and reminded me of bar fights I had witnessed during my years of military service. I thought, "This is Sunday morning, this is the church!" I separated them, called a truce and made my way into the service. I was so distraught I could not focus. My wife later told me that during the entire worship service I looked flushed and flustered. The students led the congregation through the singing and Scripture readings. I stumbled my way through the sermon. The celebration of the Lord's Supper was last. I found myself unable to participate, but I watched that elder and the preacher's wife take the cup and the bread, seemingly without any thought of their broken relationship or the ungodly things they had said to one another. The enemy attacked that morning and won the skirmish.

Believers must understand the universality and the comprehensiveness of this war. It is not just fought in random little pockets. The devil is an all-in warrior. He is our true enemy. The heavens, the mind and the church are his global battle fronts.

The third spiritual warfare principle is this war is being fought against three primary enemies. For the Jesus follower, the three enemies are the world, the flesh and the devil. These three enemies form an unholy trinity of evil. They conspire to lure every pilgrim off the path that leads to wholeness and Christlikeness.

The first enemy; the world, is a term pervasive in the Gospel of John and the Letters of John. Good Bible students know that the meaning of the word *world* very much depends on its context and how it is used by the author. When I think of the world as an enemy, the wise words of David Jackman come to mind:

> "The fact is that the word cosmos has different shades of meaning in Scripture. Sometimes it stands for the natural world which God has created—planet earth… So the 'world' comes to mean the whole human race, who are both the apex of the created order and, at the same, God's vice-regents. This is the world that God loves enough to send his Son to rescue (John 3:16). But there is another meaning of the world in the New Testament. Sometimes the world is seen as an organized system of human civilization and activity which is opposed to God and alienated from him. It represents everything that prevents man from loving, and therefore obeying, his creator."[63]

The world, as an enemy of God, represents an all-pervasive mood and atmosphere of rebellion. 1 John 2:15-16 is a key text in describing this enemy. John wrote: "Do not love the world or the things in the world. For all that is in the world—the desires of the flesh, the desires of the eyes and the pride of life—is not from the Father but is from the world." Eugene Peterson

---
63. David Jackman, *The Bible Speaks Today: The Message of John's Letters* (Downers Grove, IL: IVP, 1988), 60.

translates those same lines in *The Message*: "Don't love the world's ways. Don't love the world's goods. Love of the world squeezes out love for the Father. Practically everything that goes on in the world—wanting your own way, wanting everything for yourself, wanting to appear important—has nothing to do with the Father." John mentions "the world" six times in that passage. So, in this context, the world is the human-centered aspects of society that are under the influence, the power and the control of evil and the evil one.

The world, in the above 1 John passage, puts the emphasis on shortcuts and instant gratification. It flaunts materialism. It extols rationalism. It exalts naturalism. Our Western culture makes us quick to fight over any infringements on our freedoms. We want to be autonomous and we resist being told what to do. We crave status, and anchor ourselves in self-sufficiency. Let's call it what John calls it—the outer conflict.

The primary mark of the world is the way it distorts legitimate needs. From the world's point of view, a legitimate need can be procured in an illegitimate way. Perhaps it is why G.K. Chesterton, the brilliant British Christian of the late nineteenth and early twentieth century (1874-1936), said that men are knocking at the door of the prostitute's house not looking for sex, but looking for God. Think of Ecclesiastes 3:11. The writer states that God "put eternity into man's heart." There is, as some have observed, a God-shaped vacuum, a divine hole in all of us. This is a significant interior piece that only God can fill, and all the shortcuts in the world will not fill that void.

When I was a small boy, we had multi-piece jigsaw puzzles in our home. I enjoyed trying to put them back together. I would get to the last few pieces, and if they did not fit, I'd get a knife from my mother's kitchen utensil drawer and carve them up until they fit. Many people live life that way; deciding that they will manipulate the pieces of their lives to try to fill their God-shaped void. The world encourages such manipulation, but it will not succeed.

The second enemy in this spiritual war is the flesh: our sin dominated nature. Again, I agree with an astute observation by G. K. Chesterton. He believed that the one thing we don't need any proof about is our fallen humanity. Again, according to 1 John 2: 15-16 we have these three appetites or desires. First, we have the lust of the eyes; the desire that says, "I want what I see." When our oldest daughter was little, she used to say, "I wants that. I gots to have that, Daddy." She saw it and she wanted it. That is the lust of the eyes. It is the appeal of material things. It is the temptation to acquire. Our garages, attics and closets preach to us about accumulated stuff. So many things that we thought were vital to our life and critical to our well-being are now gathering dust. Years ago, my wife and I memorized 1 Peter 2:11 as a reminder of the war we wage against our own flesh. Peter said: "Beloved, I urge you as sojourners and exiles to abstain from the passions of the flesh, which wage war against the soul."

The third enemy, obviously, is the devil. He is the mastermind behind the world and the flesh. He is the primary influence of deception. The devil is not omnipotent. He does not share in God's all-consuming power. He is not omniscient, nor is he omnipresent. But he is far more than a symbol for evil. If we think of him as someone we can defeat on our own, we have not only made him too small, but we have made ourselves too big.

As a side note, the church universal has historically viewed the devil's attacks through the lenses of money, sex and power. This is accurate, but Satan delights in sabotaging other essential areas. He loves to distort or warp our understanding of God's grace. He wants us to believe that our sin is too great for God's grace. He loves to tyrannize us. There are many whom the evil one has convinced that God's love for them and the finished work of Christ on the cross are somehow insufficient to address their sin. What a lie! This view of Christ's atonement is undernourished and anemic. The grace of God not only is sufficient to save us; it is sufficient to change us into Christ's likeness.

Another way the devil terrorizes us is through disunity and broken relationships. He loves it when we are superficial, judgmental, and harsh toward others. He rejoices when we are fearful of others. He celebrates when we fail to intercede for one another and encourage one another. He hates genuine Christian community. Dietrich Bonhoeffer said it so well:

> "A Christian fellowship lives and exists by the intercession of its members for one another, or it collapses. I can no longer condemn or hate a brother for whom I pray, no matter how much trouble he causes me… To make intercession means to grant our brother the same right that we have received, namely, to stand before Christ and share in his mercy."[64]

The fourth and final spiritual warfare principle is that this war has already been won. The evil one doesn't want us to believe this, and wants to convince us of one of two lies. His first lie is that there is no war: no cosmic battle between the forces of good and the forces of evil. If he cannot convince us of that, his second lie is that this war is one that we cannot win. But take heart. The truth is that we are already on the winning side. Christ is always the victor!

The great theologians of a generation ago thought of World War II and the D-Day landing at Normandy as the perfect metaphor for the Jesus-following life and our ultimate victory in Christ. June 6, 1944, broke the back of Nazi Germany and its allies. Yes, the war continued. My own father was captured and imprisoned during that time. Yet as we look back on that horrible global war, the turning point was D-Day. For Christ-followers, AD 33 was our D-Day. Our Lord, on the cross, defeated sin, death and the devil

---

64. Dietrich Bonhoeffer, *Life Together* (New York, NY: Harper and Row, 1954), 86.

and secured our victory. Yes, spiritual war continues. Yes, skirmishes go on between the forces of darkness and light, but the ultimate outcome of the war has been decided.

The thought of that glorious triumph always makes me think of C.S. Lewis' classic scene in *The Lion, The Witch and the Wardrobe*. The White Witch had bargained with Aslan over the life of Edmund. Aslan had willingly offered his life in place of the boy's. The Witch and her minions had shaved Aslan's mane, muzzled him, bound him with ropes and placed him on the flat stone. It was then that the Witch said to Aslan:

> "And now, who has won? Fool, did you think that by all this you would save the human traitor? Now I will kill you instead of him as our pact was and so the Deep Magic will be appeased. But when you are dead what will prevent me from killing him as well? And who will take him out of my hand then? Understand that you have given me Narnia forever, you have lost your own life and you have not saved his. In that knowledge, despair and die."[65]

Aslan, of course, died, but the dawn brought a Narnia-shattering outcome that the White Witch could have never imagined. Lucy and Susan, with the rising of the sun, noticed the great stone slab was "broken into two pieces by a great crack that ran down it from end to end; and there was no Aslan… There, shining in the sunrise, larger than they had seen him before, shaking his mane, for it had apparently grown again, stood Aslan himself."[66] He lived again! As Lewis wrote, "Death itself would start working backward."[67] Because of our great King's victory, our soul's house is safe and under His eternal protection, even though the war continues. No other security system is needed. Praise His name!

---

65. C.S. Lewis, *The Lion, The Witch, and the Wardrobe* (New York, NY: Harper-Collins, 1994), 155.
66. Ibid., 162.
67. Ibid., 163.

CHAPTER 11

HURRY SICKNESS AND INFORMATION OVERLOAD IN THE HOUSE

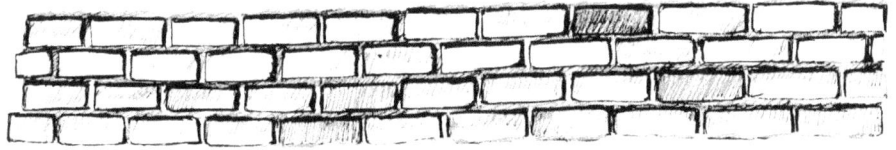

> *"Don't confuse your meals with your life, and your clothes with your body. Don't lose your head over what perishes. Nearly everything does perish: so face the facts, don't rush after the transient and unreal. Maintain your soul in tranquil dependence on God; don't worry; don't mistake what you possess for what you are. Accumulating things is useless... The simpler your house, the easier it will be to run... Thus a certain slowing down and spacing out of our ceaseless clockwork activities is a necessary condition of the deepening and enrichment of life. The spirit of joy and the spirit of hurry cannot live in the same house."* [68]

We often find ourselves driven toward hurry and disorder. We are restless, not rest-full. Many good and wise Christian spiritual directors have acknowledged this truth, and have given helpful counsel. Here are the insightful words of John Koessler, chair and professor of pastoral studies at

---

68. Underhill, *Concerning the Inner Life*, 92 and 108.

Moody Bible Institute, to Christ followers:

> "Today's congregation is a frenetic place. Our worship is marked by frenzied devotion that has full congregational participation as its primary goal. The drummer marks the tempo for the first song and we stand to sing. We remain standing through the entire song service. We are urged to lift our hands or clap in an approach to worship that sees it as a full-body experience. Between songs the worship leader tells us to fan out and find someone to whom we can introduce ourselves. The pastor reminds us to stop by the information desk and sign up for the latest congregational project and then spend time chatting over coffee with someone in the vestibule… Every week the pastor urges the congregation toward greater exertion. Congregants are told that they must round the bases from mere attendance to full involvement. They are Christ's hands and feet… What the church needs is rest. But it is a special kind of rest. We need the rest that only Christ can provide."[69]

I will come to that specific kind of "Jesus rest" momentarily. In the meantime, the words of Tish Harrison Warren, a gifted and articulate contemporary author, make a confession that any one of us could make. She tells of a time when she found herself stuck in traffic. She speaks for all of us as she describes her frustration and irritation:

> "In the face of our powerlessness, our stuckness, our mortal minutes counting down, we just honk: an act of rage and protest that only adds noise, not movement. We're geese, caught in a trap, honking. I judge the people who honk in traffic, but if my feelings made sounds they'd be honking too. I am impatient. I live in an instant world where I like to think I am the captain of the clock. I live with the illusion that time—my time at least—is something I control… In my frenetic life, I forget how to slow down and wait… For the good of my own soul I need to feel what it's like to wait, to let the moments march past. And here I am, plunged into

---
69. John Koessler, *The Radical Pursuit of Rest* (Downers Grove, IL: IVP, 2016), 18, 21-22.

an ancient spiritual practice in the middle of the freeway—forced, against my will, to practice waiting."[70]

None of us likes to feel stuck. We are in a hurry: adrenaline junkies. I am drawn to authors like Alan Fadling who admits that he is a recovering fast-pace addict and is now trying to help the rest of us admit it and do something about it. Fadling confesses:

> "I have learned, and perhaps I have been trained, that the faster I go, the more things I get done… Hurry rushes toward the destination and fails to enjoy the journey… We have a bias toward hurry. Ours is a culture that values speed, efficiency and quickness. Waiting is bad. Getting what we want now is good… I find that when I am most hurried, I run past much that God is trying to show me, give me, lead me into. Hurry becomes my automatic-pilot modus operandi rather than a way to thrive in this life. I'm learning, as I watch Jesus' unhurried way, that keeping in step with him, living with him at a walking pace, is a way to sink into and enjoy the abundant life in him that he wants me to know. So the question I would pose is this: If we are followers of an unhurried Savior, what should our pace of life look like?"[71]

As Christ followers, we know that our pace should look like the pace of Jesus, but living in this hyperlinked time causes us to feel overwhelmed, separated from others, and always in a rush. A nine-book series from the Barna Group that is highly readable and concise includes a helpful book entitled *The Hyperlinked Life* by Jun Young and David Kinnaman. Their astute insight includes this:

> "These days, you probably find yourself with less time than ever. Everything seems like it's moving at a faster pace—except

---

70. Tish Harrison Warren, *Liturgy of the Ordinary* (Downers Grove, IL: IVP, 2016), 102-103.
71. Alan Fadling, *An Unhurried Life* (Downers Grove, IL: IVP, 2013), 10-11, 16.

> your ability to keep up. Somehow, you are weighed down with more obligations than you have ever had before. Life feels more complicated. More complex... Around the world, in the next twenty-four hours, humans will text 188 billion times, send 144 billion emails, google 4.7 billion times, download 30 million apps, Skype for 2 billion minutes, write 2.1 million blog posts, and tweet 400 million times... So, the concern, then, is how to live within it—and as Christians, how to live in it well. We believe that to do so will require a theology of information. What do we mean by that? We are referring to a deep and livable understanding of how God intends for humans to interact with the tools and information now so readily available."[72]

Because many of us can work everywhere, we find that rest, silence and solitude cannot be found anywhere. How can the soul's house survive the pandemic of hurry sickness and information overload? Believe it or not, there is an antidote offered by Jesus in Matthew 11:28-30. Offered in a context of prayer, Jesus said this:

> "Come to me all who labor and are heavy laden, and I will give you rest. Take my yoke upon you, and learn from me for I am gentle and lowly in heart, and you will find rest for your souls. For my yoke is easy and my burden is light."

Many of us have found Eugene Peterson's translation of these words refreshing and insightful. Peterson put it like this in *The Message:*

> "Are you tired? Worn out? Burned out on religion? Come to me. Get away with me and you'll recover your life. I'll show you how to take a real rest. Walk with me and work with me—watch how I do it. Learn the unforced rhythms of grace. I won't lay anything heavy or ill-fitting on you. Keep company with me and you'll learn to live freely and lightly."

---

72. Jun Young and David Kinnaman, *The Hyperlinked Life: Live with Wisdom in an Age of Information Overload*, Frames—Barna Group (Grand Rapids, MI: Zondervan, 2013), 7, 30, 32.

Jesus offered a five-part, upside-down, paradoxical antidote in this passage. Let me label the first part as **our soul's invitation**. Jesus said, "Come to me." The person of Christ saturates this passage with His use of first-person language. I, me and my are reminders that He alone can provide what we really need. Jesus' gentle words, "Come to me," are not a command. They are an invitation to our soul. He literally says, "Come here, please. Come where I am." This is the same grammatical construction used in other places in Matthew—when Jesus called the disciples, taught a parable and when the angel of the Lord told Mary Magdalene and the other Mary to look into the empty tomb of Jesus (4:19, 25:34, and 28:6). My favorite use of this same language in the New Testament is found in John 21:12. At the post-resurrection beach breakfast prepared by our Lord, Jesus beckoned to the disciples, saying, "Come and have breakfast." Jesus said to those first disciples what he says to us now: "Come here, please."

Any of us who are burdened with rule-keeping and legalism can find an antidote for our soul's house in Jesus' gentle words. Any of us weighed down by life's pace and the pressures that have been placed upon us can find a Savior who is able to bear the weight as He offers His sweet invitation. Craig Blomberg explains Jesus' invitation this way by writing:

> "All may come, at least all who hurt and who recognize their spiritual need… The invitation to come to Christ remains for all today, but now as then it requires the recognition that persons cannot come by exalting themselves, but only be completely depending on and trusting in Christ."[73]

Frederick Bruner adds this insight. He writes:

> "Jesus does not say, 'Come to God' and receive these promises. Instead, quite in line with his remarks in this chapter and throughout

---

73. Craig Blomberg, *Matthew* (Nashville, TN: Broadman Press, 1992), 194-195.

the Gospel, Jesus presents himself as the fully authorized representative of God… Without any mitigating explanation, Jesus invites all troubled persons to himself… In Jesus, God gets a face. Jesus invites us to himself, and we feel quite naturally that we are invited to God… Only a certain kind of person is invited by Jesus—just as in the previous paragraph only a certain kind of person was rebuked by Jesus. Jesus invites those who are having a hard time of it, those for whom life is hard work and who feel overwhelmed… Jesus' invitation goes out to all those for whom life has become a grind, for whom existence is laborious, to those, in a word, from whom the juice has gone out of life and all that's left is the rind. Jesus' heart goes out to them."[74]

This soul invitation reminds me of the short courtship my wife and I enjoyed. She was a senior in Bible college, and I showed up—fresh out of military service—ready to begin a long academic journey. Our lives were full of term papers, tests, and due dates. We both knew that we wanted to spend the rest of whatever life there was with each other. So we made space for one another most evenings at a nearby McDonald's. She would say to me, "Meet me there for hot chocolate and fries at 9:00 p.m." I did so, not by demand or drudgery, but in pure delight. It is with that same delight that I hear in the words of Jesus' invitation to my soul's house.

The second part of this antidote I would call **our soul's temptation.** Jesus said, "Come to me, all who labor and are heavy laden… " All of us are tempted to carry what is not ours to carry. "Labor" is the kind of work that tires us, fatigues us, and diminishes our energy. The word used by Jesus for "labor" here was a term applied to soldiers or manual laborers who were literally "struck down" by exhaustion. The other term Jesus used, "heavy laden," described someone who was weighed down and overloaded with a sizable burden. In the larger context of Jesus' teaching ministry, this same

---

[74]. Frederick Bruner, *The Christbook: Matthew 1-12*, Revised and Expanded Edition. (Grand Rapids, MI: Eerdmans, 2004), 537-538.

word is used by Jesus to describe what the Pharisees and other religious leaders did to the Jewish people. Jesus said, "For you load people with *burdens hard to bear*, and you yourselves do not touch the *burdens* with one of your fingers" (Luke 11:46). Jesus came to take on all of our labor and burden. We think we can carry some part of the load but David Platt is right. Jesus wants all of it. Platt writes:

> "Jesus called the weary and burdened to come to him. This is Christianity explained: we give him the full weight of all our sin. These people were so burdened because they had failed over and over again to keep the law, and as leaders poured on more laws, the people felt more guilty. The weight of their sin became heavier, and they could not stand up under it. When Jesus calls us to give him the weight of all our sin, we don't merely give him some of it, but rather all of it. And it's not just the weight of our sin that we give to Jesus; we give him our complete and utter inability to obey God… The call to come to Christ is definitively not a call to try and reform your life and to be a better person—that's not Christianity."[75]

Hurry sickness and information overload is symptomatic of our sin and our lives in a sin-fractured world. The antidote does not rest in self-improvement plans or muscling our way through seasons of stress and pressure. We Jesus followers are not to be a driven people. We are a called people. We are a surrendered people, not those enslaved.

The third part of the antidote I would label as **our soul's satisfaction.** "*Rest*" is the word Jesus used. He said, "I will give you *rest*" and "You will find *rest* for your souls." Rest is not a difficult word to understand. Rest implies "refreshment" or "to take a needed break." The word calls us back to Genesis 2:2, where God applied rest to His own rhythm. The Scripture

---

[75]. David Platt, *Christ-Centered Exposition: Exalting Jesus in Matthew* (Nashville, TN: B&H Publishing, 2013), 152.

says: "And on the seventh day God finished His work that He had done, and *He rested* on the seventh day from all His work that He had done." In the unfolding Gospel story, rest is more than just a day. Rest is comprehensive in the Scriptures. It includes a specific day, the Sabbath, but it is also portrayed as a regular practice we enter (Exodus 20:8-11). It is a posture: a position of submission (Mark 6:31). Even more, it is a place that we are promised (Hebrews 3-4). Finally, rest is a person. Jesus alone gives the rest that Moses and Joshua could not. Our soul's house is satisfied by the rest Jesus provided at the cross and continues to provide now, as He lives in us.

Rest teaches us the unforced rhythms of grace. It is the way we learn to keep company with Jesus. It is the way we learn to live freely and lightly. Rest is both now and not yet. We anticipate the rest that Revelation 14:13 describes. "Blessed are the dead who die in the Lord from now on. 'Blessed indeed,' says the Spirit, that they may *rest* from their labors, for their deeds follow them!" I love the description of rest that Matthew Sleeth, a former emergency room physician, offers in his beautiful book, *24/6: A Prescription for a Healthier, Happier Life:*

> "Rest is stopping one's work, whatever that work may be. Rest is freedom from harassment. It is the quiet after the storm. It is children fresh out of a bath with pruned fingers and the smell of baby shampoo, tucked under their blankets before bedtime. Rest is the song of the night breeze rattling the palms as it comes in off the Gulf. Rest is putting your head down on the pillow knowing that you can sleep in. Rest is the beast of burden unhitched from the plow. Rest is walking around the edge of shorn cornfields in the fall. Rest is reading and setting the book aside when your eyes get too heavy. Rest is the song of the wind through the screen porch of the beach house. Rest is stopping. It is staring up through the thin Colorado night sky at the spine of our galaxy. Rest is thinking about all the things that you could do on a Sunday afternoon and hearing a still, small voice tell you to just stop—

and then taking a God-ordained nap… In learning how to rest, we actually gain knowledge of Christ. We learn to be gentle and humble and to give up our pride."[76]

Dr. Sleeth tells a small part of his own journey toward soul satisfaction in *24/6*. He admitted that he had sworn off sentimental and superstitious things like God when he was in his twenties. Matthew and Nancy married against their parents' wishes. They went to college and then medical school. They had children, pursued success, built a nice home and made money. And then it happened. He writes:

> "More than a decade into my career, I started working at a hospital where they put me in charge… That time of life was difficult. It was filled with loss and tragedy. I realized for the first time that there was evil afoot in the world. To quote Dante, 'In the middle of the journey of our life I came to my senses in a dark forest, for I had lost the straight path.' Because of my work schedule, I began taking every Saturday off. This wasn't for any spiritual reason, but merely to shepherd strength for the next day's twenty-four-hour shift. I decided not to go shopping or to do projects around the house and instead took walks, read, and rested. I also sought answers in new places. Most of the books I had read were silent on the subjects of good and evil, so I began investigating the world's great sacred texts, starting with the Hindu epics— The Ramayana and the Bhagavad Gita. Then one slow Sunday afternoon at the hospital, I spotted a Bible on a waiting room table. I picked it up. I had never read it, and we didn't have one at home. So I stole it. I studied the New Testament and encountered Jesus. My life has never been the same. I tell this story not to illustrate my conversion to Christianity, but to show what can happen when someone stops working one day a week… I believe that God gave the Fourth Commandment so that we could grapple with the number of our days. When I slowed to a stop, I became intensely curious about what happens—spiritually, not

---

76. Matthew Sleeth, *24/6: A Prescription for a Healthier, Happier Life* (Carol Stream, IL: Tyndale, 2012), 83-85.

just physically—when someone dies. I wanted to know if life mattered. I began to number my days."[77]

Our soul's satisfaction is located only in Christ. This awareness leads to a fourth part of our antidote for hurry sickness and information overload. I would label this as **our soul's participation.** Jesus said, "Take my yoke upon you and learn from me." He said, "My yoke is easy and my burden is light." The word "yoke" is not one that many of us spend much time thinking about. In ancient times, a yoke was a cross beam made of wood or iron. It joined two animals together to enable them to work together in unity. For many, it is an image of subjection, and bondage—forced submission. The Old Testament prophet, Jeremiah, was told by God to make a yoke and put it on his own neck as a symbol of Judah's captivity and submission to Babylon and King Nebuchadnezzar (Jeremiah 27:2). Here, Jesus took a very negative image and made it a very positive one.

Consider this: a yoke is a walking tool. As Jesus invited His first disciples, He now invites us to walk where He walks and learn from Him. The yoke becomes the instrument through which Jesus teaches us how to live, how to keep company with Him and how to do His work in His way. Jesus' words about yokes is expanded in a story from the life of Justin Martyr (100-165 AD). Around 132 AD or so, Justin had a conversation with a Jewish man by the name of Trypho who was searching for truth in philosophy. Justin asked him why he was searching there instead of his own Scriptures. Years later, Justin wrote about how Christians were praying that Abraham's descendants would recognize Jesus for who He was and would, of their own free choice, respond in faith. Justin recalled what he had said to Trypho:

> "And when Jesus came to the Jordan, being supposed to be the son of Joseph the carpenter, and appearing without form as

---

77. Sleeth, *24/6*, 99-100.

the Scriptures proclaimed, and supposed to be a carpenter—for when He lived among men He wrought these works of a carpenter, ploughs and yokes, teaching by them both the signs of righteousness and a life of energy—the Holy Spirit fluttered down on Him in the form of a dove."[78]

Justin wanted Trypho to know that in Jesus, philosophy finds its completion. Jesus Christ, the promised Messiah, invites any and all into a unique participation of delightful yoke sharing. The reliable Leon Morris describes all of this so well:

"Paradoxically those who take Christ's yoke on them have rest, rest now and eternal rest in the hereafter. Jesus adds a sentence that shows that the service to which He calls is no difficult and burdensome affair. His yoke is easy… He does not call people to a burdensome and worrying existence… It adds up to an invitation to service indeed; Jesus is not calling people to lives of careless ease. But it is service for which they will be glad. It will be a delight, not a painful drudgery."[79]

In a way that I cannot entirely explain, the yoke of Jesus is a life preserver. His yoke keeps us from drowning in the ocean of an untethered life. Busyness and mental overload are dangers to our soul's house. Kevin DeYoung reminds us that hectic living can ruin our joy, rob our hearts and cover up the rot in our souls. Kevin says, "What we need is the Great Physician to heal our over-scheduled souls."[80] Jesus offers us His yoke.

A fifth and final part of the antidote for hurry sickness and information overload can be found in Jesus' words: "I am gentle and lowly in heart." I would label this as **our soul's preoccupation.** A healthy soul is preoccupied

---

78. Justin Martyr, *Justin Martyr: The Dialogue with Trypho*, trans. A. Lukyn Williams (New York, NY: MacMillan Company, 1930), 189-190.
79. Leon Morris, *The Gospel According to Matthew* (Grand Rapids, MI: Eerdmans, 1992), 297.
80. Kevin DeYoung, *Crazy Busy* (Wheaton, IL: Crossway, 2013), 32.

with this gentle and lowly Savior. Good Bible students have observed that this is the only place in Scripture where Jesus tells us about His own heart. I am drawn to the clear and compelling way Dane Ortlund explains this statement from Jesus:

> "In the one place in the Bible where the Son of God pulls back the veil and lets us peer way down into the core of who he is, we are not told that he is 'austere and demanding in heart.' We are not told that he is 'exalted and dignified in heart.' We are not even told that he is 'joyful and generous in heart.' Letting Jesus set the terms, his surprising claim is that he is 'gentle and lowly in heart'… Meek. Humble. Gentle. Jesus is not trigger-happy. Not harsh, reactionary, easily exasperated. He is the most understanding person in the universe… The meaning of the word 'lowly' overlaps with that of 'gentle,' together communicating a single reality about Jesus's heart… The point in saying that Jesus is lowly is that he is accessible. For all his resplendent glory and dazzling holiness, his supreme uniqueness and otherness, no one in human history has ever been more approachable than Jesus Christ. No prerequisites. No hoops to jump through… This is who he is for those who come to him, who take his yoke upon them, who cry to him for help."[81]

All of this gentle and lowly talk points us to the undeniable truth that God's grace cannot be exhausted. Any misconceived or warped view of what God is like is corrected and replaced with a Savior who is immeasurably approachable. If we want to purge our soul's house of anything that reeks of legalism, drivenness, hurry sickness, information overload and any other do-it-yourself religious living, then we must submit to the goodness of Jesus. He alone is all-supreme and all-sufficient. As upside-down as it sounds, we find freedom by submitting to Christ's yoke.

Years ago, my wife and I were invited to dinner and a movie by a couple

---

81. Ortlund, *Gentle and Lowly*, 18-21.

who were seeking to understand the claims of Christ on their marriage and especially on their individual lives. The couple owned a beautiful cottage-like house on the campus of the University of Illinois. After serving us a splendid meal, we watched the award-winning film, *The Mission.* The array of stars in that film included Robert De Niro, Jeremy Irons and Liam Neeson. De Niro played a mercenary slave trader, Rodrigo Mendoza, who enslaved and sold the Guarani indigenous peoples of South America. In a fit of jealous rage, Mendoza killed his brother and then faced the horror of what he had done. He could not forgive himself. Father Gabriel, a Jesuit priest played by Jeremy Irons, exhorted Mendoza to do penance by dragging a large net filled with things that represented his past life—his sword, armor, other weapons—and to go to the very people he had enslaved and sold. In a scene that I will never forget, other Jesuits tried to help Mendoza carry the weight and burden from his past life but in the end, only the Guarani could give Rodrigo Mendoza the assistance and forgiveness that he needed to receive. They alone could cut the heavy burden from his shoulders and push it into the river below. There was much more to the movie, but the scene of Mendoza's repentance and the Guaranis' forgiveness has been permanently seared into my heart and soul. It reminds me that my soul's invitation, temptation, satisfaction, participation, and preoccupation all find their peace in the freeing yoke of Jesus.

Only Jesus provides the necessary antidote to any and all forms of hurry sickness and overload that enter the soul's house. Evelyn Underhill said it well: "The spirit of joy and the spirit of hurry cannot live in the same house."[82] Genuine Christian spiritual formation is both an abandonment and an attachment. We abandon hurry and attach ourselves to the restful yoke of Jesus.

---

82. Underhill, *Concerning the Inner Life*, 108.

CHAPTER 12

THE SOUL HOUSE'S QUEST

> *"What is the final need of our ground-floor premises, if they are to bear the weight of the upper story; the thrust and pressure of the supernatural life? The Saints reply, with one voice: Fortitude, strength, staying-power!"*[83]

Anyone who has ever owned a house knows the relentless need for repairs. A homeowner has to have grit. Upkeep can include a new roof, a new furnace, a fresh coat of paint, plumbing repairs, updated furnishings, and on and on. Similarly, the soul's house requires ongoing restoration. Evelyn Underhill correctly understood that fortitude would be required. The primary quest of the soul's house is to know Christ. No Bible passage challenges me and compels me in this pursuit more than Philippians 3:7-16. Here is what Paul wrote to the Jesus-followers at Philippi:

> But whatever gain I had, I counted as loss for the sake of Christ. Indeed, I count everything as loss because of the surpassing worth of knowing Christ Jesus my Lord. For his sake I have suffered the loss of all things and count them as rubbish,

---
83. Underhill, *Concerning the Inner Life*, 99.

in order that I may gain Christ and be found in him, not having a righteousness of my own that comes from the law, but that which comes through faith in Christ, the righteousness from God that depends on faith—that I may know him and the power of his resurrection, and may share his sufferings, becoming like him in his death, that by any means possible I may attain the resurrection from the dead.

Not that I have already obtained this or am already perfect, but I press on to make it my own, because Christ Jesus has made me his own. Brothers, I do not consider that I have made it my own. But one thing I do: forgetting what lies behind and straining forward to what lies ahead, I press on toward the goal for the prize of the upward call of God in Christ Jesus. Let those of us who are mature think this way, and if in anything you think otherwise, God will reveal that also to you. Only let us hold true to what we have attained.

The fundamental question that Philippians 3:7-16 asks is this: What does it mean to know Christ? This glorious obsession to know Him makes me think about how I know my wife, Sue. I met her in August 1976 as she was entering her senior year of college after a summer of service and recruitment for Lincoln Christian University. I'd met her brother, Chris, in the college enrollment line a few days earlier, and he invited me to join both of them for a Coke. I initially had declined, but at the last minute I joined them. I sat while they talked. Sue would tell you that I hardly said a word the entire evening. She thought I was too quiet, and I thought she talked too much. Yet I found myself looking for excuses to see her. Our courtship was quick and before 1976 ended, I asked Sue to marry me. Sunday, June 26, 1977, we said our vows and began life together as husband and wife. We worked at our marriage. We spent large blocks of time together and listened to each other. We laughed. We cried. We hoped. We took walks. We planted a garden. We cooked. We cleaned. We took time to pray, plan and dream. We were intentional about prioritizing our marriage, even when our sweet children entered the picture. We did not always get things right, but we embraced knowing one another fully. That sacred commitment continues to this day. I know her, but go on knowing her. She still surprises me, from time to time, with the beauty of her life and heart.

In a similar way, we can know Christ as we go on knowing Him. The great J.I. Packer (1926-2020) described this ongoing knowledge better than most anyone I know. He wrote these beautiful words in his classic book, *Knowing God,* back in 1973:

> "What were we made for? To know God. What aim should we set ourselves in life? To know God. What is the 'eternal life' Jesus gives? Knowledge of God. 'This is eternal life, that they might know thee, the only true God, and Jesus Christ, whom thou hast sent' (John 17:3). What is the best thing in life, bringing more joy, delight, and contentment than anything else? Knowledge of God… What we have said at once provides a foundation, shape, and goal for our lives, plus a principle of priorities and a scale of values. Once you become aware that the main business that you are here for is to know God, most of life's problems fall into place of their own accord."[84]

So again, we ask ourselves, "What does it mean to know Christ?" Paul provided at least four significant formational answers. Here is the first: **To know Christ means that Jesus is my greatest love.** If I truly know Christ, no love exceeds my love for Him. My highest devotion is to Him. With that premier love settled, all other loves find their appropriate place. I can love Sue as she deserves and desires. I can love my children, my son-in-law and my grandchildren in the way that they deserve and desire. I can love my siblings, my extended family, my friends, my colleagues, and people everywhere, when Jesus is given my heart's supreme affection. All of this

---

84. Packer, *Knowing God,* 29.

becomes abundantly clear when I understand Philippians 3:7-8.

Paul used economic language of loss and gain to describe the preeminent love he had for Christ. He counted everything a loss next to the matchless love he had for Jesus Christ. Paul's list of loss included aspects of his life previously held in high regard: circumcision, national and tribal pride, personal righteousness, membership in the Pharisaical fraternity, zeal for God and all aspects of his pre-Christ life. Paul's discarded "rubbish" was everything he had valued previously. The late Fred Craddock perfectly explained Paul's loss-profit-rubbish talk:

> "Paul does not say Judaism is worthless, that it is refuse (garbage or excrement), that way of life is not of value. What he is describing is his consuming desire to know Jesus Christ, to be in Jesus Christ, to have that righteousness which is God's gift to the one who believes; and for the surpassing worth of that, he counts gain as loss. It is not the law that is dead; Paul is dead to the law. Paul does not toss away junk to gain Christ; he tosses away that which was of tremendous value to him… What Paul is saying is that Christ surpasses everything of worth to me."[85]

Jesus alone was Paul's "pearl of great value" (Matthew 13:45-46). I can testify to this exchange of loss and gain at a deeply personal level. Since I met Jesus, and have experienced the "born again" life (John 3:5-8), anything that I have surrendered cannot compare to what I have received. My life is a new creation found only in Christ (2 Corinthians 5:17). If Jesus Christ is my greatest love, time with Him will be my greatest priority. Anyone who loves someone spends time with that one.

I have mentioned the priorities that love demands in other writings. Not that long ago, I asked my wife, daughters, son-in-law, and grandchildren: "How can I be a better husband, father, father-in-law and grandfather?"

---

[85]. Fred Craddock, *Philippians: Interpretation A Bible Commentary for Teaching and Preaching* (Atlanta, GA: John Knox Press, 1985), 58.

One should not ask such a question unless one is willing to wholeheartedly embrace the answer. Without manipulation or coercion, the members of my beloved family all gave the same answer to my question: "Spend time with us." So it is with Jesus.

This leads to a second answer to our central question: What does it mean to know Christ? **To know Christ means that I trust what Jesus has done for me, not what I do for Him.** Paul made this a fundamental faith issue in Philippians 3:9. He had no righteousness of his own. All of his law keeping could never make him right before God. The righteousness that he embraced was the righteousness found solely in Christ through faith. This is central to knowing Christ. I do not know Christ if I trust in my own goodness and rule keeping. If I say that I know Christ, I mean that I trust what He did for me at the cross entirely. I resonate with the way Craddock described this non-self-improvement life:

> "At the risk of excessive repetition, a summary statement seems in order here. There are two kinds of religious experience with many adherents which do not have their scriptural support in Philippians 3:4-9. One is that which finds Christianity a better religion, and therefore attractive to anyone always on the lookout for improvement of one's station, fortune, and peace of mind, not to mention prospects in the hereafter… The other kind of religious experience not supported by this text is that which views the past as totally negative, a failure in every way. Certainly there are those who become Christian out of a background of confused values, wasted opportunities, inner turmoil, and social wreckage. This fact is not be denied nor treated lightly; but that pattern is not to be imposed upon the portrait of a man at war with himself, crucified between the sky of God's expectations and the earth of his own paltry performance. Paul is not in this scene a poor soul standing with a grade of ninety-nine before a God who counts one hundred as the lowest passing grade."[86]

---

86. Craddock, *Philippians*, 58-59.

Paul trusted in the righteousness of God, found in the gift of Christ at the cross, not in his own adherence to the law. His faith was in Christ alone. All who truly want to know Christ, must place their faith in Christ alone. "Faith" (*pistis*) is a foundational formational word. Without it, there is not ongoing transformation. The word occurs sixty-seven times in the New Testament, nearly half in Paul's letters. I love the simple insight of Harold Moulton. He wrote: "God's nature is the heart of the New Testament meaning of *pistis*. Because God is utterly reliable and trustworthy, men can put their whole faith and trust in Him."[87]

I had the opportunity to hear Brennan Manning (1934-2013) speak in Indianapolis years ago. He was in the process of writing his superb book *Ruthless Trust*. He told the story of a missionary family furloughed in the United States and staying at the lake house of a friend. The mom and dad were busy doing chores and their three children (ages four, seven and twelve) were playing on the dock. Suddenly, the twelve-year old screamed. Four-year old Billy had fallen into eight feet of water. Dad dove into the lake, but could not locate his son. Several attempts failed but finally, the father located his son deep in the water clinging to one of the wooden pier posts. Once safely in his dad's arms and on dry land, he was asked, "'Billy, what were you doing down there?' The little one replied, 'Just waiting on you, Dad, just waiting on you.'"[88] That little boy trusted in his dad's love and faithfulness. He knew his father would come to his rescue. Manning made his point: "Ruthless trust ultimately comes down to this: faith in the person of Jesus and hope in his promise… It doesn't get any more ruthless. Either we believe in the resurrection and therefore trust in Jesus of Nazareth and the gospel he preached, or we do not believe in the resurrection and therefore do

---

87. Harold Moulton, *The Challenge of the Concordance* (London, GB: Hollen Street Press, 1977), 271.
88. Brennan Manning, *Ruthless Trust* (San Francisco, CA: Harper-Collins, 2000), 95-96.

not trust in Jesus of Nazareth and the gospel he preached."[89]

This trust conviction leads to a third answer to what it means to know Christ. Third, **to know Christ means that I go on knowing Jesus, regardless of the cost**. For Paul, the resurrection and suffering for Jesus were central to knowing Him. Paul's word order in Philippians 3:10 is essential to our ongoing movement into Christ's likeness. He first described the resurrection, then suffering and finally death. We tend to think death, resurrection and life. What Paul was emphasizing was cross-bearing and self-denial. His point was and is that the Jesus-following life is costly. Paul echoed what Jesus had already said: "If anyone would come after me, let him deny himself and take up his cross daily and follow me" (Matthew 16:24; Mark 8:34; and Luke 9:23).

This cost factor was evident in the life of the early disciples. In Acts 4, Peter and John were warned to stop speaking and teaching in the name of Jesus (Acts 4:17-18). Their defiant testimony was clear: "We cannot but speak of what we have seen and heard" (Acts 4:20). The apostles were arrested, beaten and "charged… not to speak in the name of Jesus" (Acts 5:40). Dr. Luke tells us that the apostles left the council, "Rejoicing that they were counted worthy to suffer dishonor for the name" (Acts 5:41). Later, Paul spoke of his own determination to suffer for Christ. He told the Ephesian elders: "But I do not account my life of any value nor as precious to myself, if only I may finish my course and the ministry that I received from the Lord Jesus, to testify to the gospel of the grace of God. And now, behold, I know that none of you among whom I have gone about proclaiming the kingdom will see my face again" (Acts 20:24-25). Paul reminded Timothy of the persecutions, suffering and inherent cost involved in knowing Christ. He said: "All who desire to live a godly life in Christ Jesus will be persecuted" (2 Timothy 3:12). The courage of those early apprentices of Jesus never wavered in their

---

89. Manning, *Ruthless Trust*, 178.

desire to know Christ and make Him known. They had counted the cost.

Many of us know the price Pastor Dietrich Bonhoeffer willingly paid during the evil reign of Adolph Hitler and the Nazi regime. Bonhoeffer said: "We must shake off the fear of this world—the cause of Christ is at stake, and we are to be found sleeping?… Christ is looking down at us and asking whether there is anyone left who confesses faith in him."[90]

Bonhoeffer was arrested and imprisoned, first at Buchenwald and then finally at Flossenburg, Germany. He was sentenced to death by hanging. History offers us the eyewitness account of Dr. H. Fischer-Hullstrung, the camp physician, who observed the last minutes of Bonhoeffer's life:

> "On the morning of that day between five and six o'clock the prisoners, among them Admiral Canaris, General Oster, General Thomas and Reichgeritsrat Sack were taken from their cells, and the verdicts of the court martial read out to them. Through the half-open door in one room of the huts I saw Pastor Bonhoeffer, before taking off his prison garb, kneeling on the floor praying fervently to his God. I was most deeply moved by the way this lovable man prayed, so devout and so certain that God heard his prayer. At the place of execution, he again said a short prayer and then climbed the steps to the gallows, brave and composed. His death ensued after a few seconds. In the almost fifty years that I worked as a doctor, I have hardly ever seen a man die so entirely submissive to the will of God."[91]

Eric Metaxas summarizes Bonhoeffer's death with these pointed words: "Bonhoeffer thought it the plain duty of the Christian—and the privilege and honor—to suffer with those who suffered."[92] To know Christ intimately requires that I know the cost of such a commitment and remain steadfast to that commitment.

---

90. Eric Metaxas, *Bonhoeffer: Pastor, Martyr, Prophet, Spy* (New York, NY: Thomas Nelson, 2010), 219.
91. Metaxes, *Bonhoeffer*, 532.
92. Metaxes, *Bonhoeffer*, 532.

Fourth and finally, **to know Christ means that I follow Jesus my whole life.** As Paul was saying in Philippians 3:11-16, he was preoccupied with knowing Christ more and more. He longed to finish well. Perhaps no one explains this better than D. A. Carson, the brilliant professor of New Testament studies:

> "For the privilege of knowing that Master better, no suffering is too great… One reason why Paul adopts this stance is because he holds the End in view: he wants to know Christ in these ways, he says, 'and so attain to the resurrection from the dead" (3:11)… And in Paul's mind, attaining that glorious end, the final resurrection, the new heaven and the new earth, the home of righteousness, is bound up with persevering in the knowledge of Jesus Christ. So for knowledge of Christ Paul yearns. In other words, Paul is not stagnating… He is pressing on. He does not think of himself as having already been made perfect. Indeed, he explicitly disavows the suggestion… What he is aiming for is the attainment of the very purpose for which Christ called him… Refusing to stand on past triumphs, Paul eagerly strains forward to the glories to come. Not for a moment is Paul suggesting that his stance is unique, or one that is expected only of apostles… The implications are staggering. Christians should never be satisfied with yesterday's grace. It is a shocking thing for Christians to have to admit that they have grown little in their knowledge of Jesus Christ."[93]

Note Paul's humility in these verses. He confessed that he had not already attained this maturity nor was already perfect (3:12). He blended two pictures of pressing on and straining forward (3:12 and 14). Paul described a wholehearted, lifelong pursuit of Jesus. Christ alone was worthy of chasing after for a lifetime. Paul's goal in pursuit and chase was to know Christ intimately. He stretched and leaned forward like a runner: hastening, perspiring, and striving, to finish the race well. Paul longed to know Christ

---
93. D.A. Carson, *Basics for Believers: An Exposition of Philippians* (Grand Rapids, MI: Baker Academic, 1996), 88-90.

better and better.

Our transformation into Jesus' likeness is shaped by our ongoing desire to know Him. But more than that, it is shaped by our Triune God's knowledge of who we are. A wise reminder is essential here. J.I. Packer put it this way:

> "What matters supremely, therefore, is not, in the last analysis, the fact that I know God, but the larger fact which underlies it—the fact that He knows me. I am graven on the palms of His hands. I am never out of His mind. All my knowledge of Him depends on His sustained initiative in knowing me. I know Him, because He first knew me, and continues to know me… This is momentous knowledge. There is unspeakable comfort in knowing that God is constantly taking knowledge of me in love and watching over me for my good… He wants me as His friend, and desires to be my friend, and has given His Son to die for me in order to realize this purpose."[94]

Those who pursue the soul house's quest to know Christ are those who discover what Paul identifies as "joy." Joy is the perfect ingredient in every house of the soul.

---

94. Packer, *Knowing God*, 37.

CHAPTER 13

THE SOUL HOUSE'S HORIZON: FORMATION'S LONG VIEW

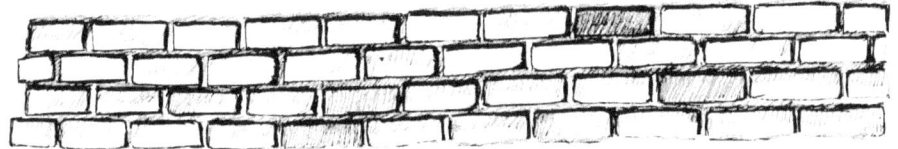

> *"Perhaps the best thing of all: as the best hours of human life are often those when the home is closed from the outside world, the curtains are drawn and the lamp lit. When the curtains of faith are drawn, we find that we are not alone in the upper room. A companion is there with us, and has always been with us; when we hardly noticed—almost took for granted—when we were gazing at the marvelous view."*[95]

I like the view I have as I walk to the Kickapoo Creek from my house. God is evident in the details of what He has created. Occasionally someone expresses my view in a way that fits like a finely tailored suit. This morning I read this line: "After all, what is spiritual formation if not developing eyes to see."[96]

Maintaining the grace necessary to see the ever-present Triune God

---

95. Underhill, *Concerning the Inner Life*, 119.
96. Amanda Iglesias, "For Those With Eyes to See, There is Theological Truth in Church Architecture," *www.christianitytoday.com*, December 8, 2021, https://www.christianitytoday.com/ct/2021/december-web-only/church-architecture-theology-read-elevation-plan-section.html.

around us is not easy. We live in the lowlands of everyday life where the haze never seems to burn away, and a cloud of smog prevents us from seeing the God who is present.

I have lived longer than I thought I would. Age causes me to ponder the long view of Christian spiritual formation. That steady look over the horizon of transformation is the practice of the presence of God throughout a lifetime. In chapter six I mentioned a term that A.W. Tozer used: "spiritual receptivity." Tozer said this: "The one vital quality… the great saints had in common was spiritual receptivity. Something in them was open to heaven, something which urged them God-ward."[97] Tozer knew that Scripture made self-evident the fact that God can be known as we know any other person, if one has been born again. God is here, yet many people are wholly unaware of Him. God is self-revealing. He wants us to know Him, see Him, hear Him and walk with Him. Tozer beautifully added:

> "The universal Presence is a fact. God is here… And always He is trying to get our attention, to reveal Himself to us, to communicate with us. We have within us the ability to know Him if we will but respond to His overtures. (And this we call pursuing!) We will know Him in increasing degree as our receptivity becomes more perfect by faith and love and practice."[98]

What matters is our alertness for God. Nicolas Herman, a French Carmelite monk, better known as Brother Lawrence (1614-1691), awakened this in me. Lawrence looked for the glory of God in the commonplace. Though physically awkward, Lawrence was spiritually alert and agile when it came to giving God complete attention. I love the summary he once offered to a woman seeking spiritual direction. I keep these words in the front of my Bible. Lawrence said of God:

---

97. Tozer, *The Pursuit of God*, 67.
98. Ibid., 71.

"Let us think of Him perpetually... How can we be with Him but in thinking of Him often? And how can we often think of Him but by a holy habit which we should form of it? You will tell me that I am always saying the same thing. It is true, for this is the best and easiest method I know; and as I use no other, I advise all the world to do it. We must know before we can love. In order to know God, we must often think of Him; and when we come to love Him, we shall also think of Him often, for our heart will be with our treasure. This is an argument which well deserves your consideration."[99]

Brother Lawrence lived his convictions by being observant in his everyday life. Much of his time was spent working mundane jobs in the monastery, often in the kitchen. His ordinary work prompted him to pray routinely: "Lord, of all pots and pans and things... Make me a saint by getting meals and washing up the plates."[100] I have placed those words beside the kitchen sink in our home. I want to be an apprentice who is fully alert to God in my everyday life. I can label this desire in so many different ways. I can label this keeping watch, paying attention, observing, cultivating wonder, holy seeing and listening, even keen awareness of how the grace of God is at work every day. Framed as a question, I ask, "Are my eyes opened and focused on the God who is present?"

At least six biblical passages remind me of the urgency of staying spiritually receptive to our Triune God. I think first of Genesis 28:10-16 and the oblivious attitude of Jacob. Fearful of his brother Esau, Jacob was somewhere near Bethel (Genesis 28:19). He slept and dreamed of a ladder that appeared where the angels of God were ascending and descending. Through that dream, God spoke to Jacob, reminding him that the promise

---

99. Brother Lawrence, *The Practice of the Presence of God with Spiritual Maxims* (Grand Rapids, MI: Fleming H. Revell, 1993), 51.
100. Lawrence, *Practice of the Presence of God*, 9.

he had made to Abraham and Isaac was now being made to him: "And in you and your offspring shall all the families of the earth be blessed… I am with you and will keep you wherever you go" (Genesis 28:14-15). When Jacob awoke, he said to himself: "Surely the LORD is in this place, and I did not know it" (Genesis 28:16). Tozer observed: "Jacob had never been for one small division of a moment outside the circle of that all-pervading Presence. But he knew it not. That was his trouble, and it is ours."[101] We Christ-followers must not go on being unaware of the ever-present God.

The second biblical passage that reminds me of our need for receptivity is 1 Samuel 3:7-10. I find Samuel's story fascinating, yet author Philip Yancey disdained this narrative because of the way his own mother had twisted this biblical story to manipulate Philip and his older brother Marshall, into believing that they had been ordained for a divine cause.[102] Yancey identified the contrast. Samuel's mother Hannah longed to have a child but was unable to conceive. In desperation and distress, she prayed to the LORD weeping bitterly. Hannah asked God to give her a son and promised that she would give him back to the LORD all the days of his life (1 Samuel 1:10-11).

God granted Hannah's heartfelt petition. Samuel was raised, weaned and given to Eli the priest at Shiloh, where the boy ministered in the House of the LORD. The story is familiar. A sleeping Samuel heard his name, and thinking it was Eli summoning him, Samuel ran to the priest and said, "Here I am, for you called me" (1 Samuel 3:5). The boy was completely unaware of God's presence, and the storyteller reminds us: "The word of the LORD was rare in those days; there was no frequent vision" (1 Samuel 3:1). This strange summons happened three times before Eli discerned that it was the LORD who was calling Samuel. Eli instructed the boy, "Go, lie down, and if he calls you, you shall say, 'Speak, LORD, for your servant hears'" (1

---
101. Tozer, *The Pursuit of God*, 64.
102. Philip Yancey, *Where the Light Fell: A Memoir* (Colorado Springs, CO: Convergent Books, 2021).

Samuel 3:9). God spoke. Samuel responded and grew in his awareness of the presence of God. The Scriptures tell us that Samuel "let none of his words fall to the ground… And the LORD appeared again at Shiloh, for the LORD revealed himself to Samuel at Shiloh by the word of the LORD" (1 Samuel 3:19-21).

Samuel is not Jacob. One is a boy and the other a grown man. Yet, both of these biblical stories help us to see the ongoing need for alertness to God's presence. Samuel, like us, had to learn to discern that Presence and voice. Thankfully, we have God's Word, and can meet with Him daily and ask Him to speak into our inner life. The upkeep and orderliness of our soul's house requires it. Yet, how often do we fail to hear Him through what he has created, through conversations with others, through seasons of heartache and disappointment and through other circumstances? Like Samuel we must learn to be spiritually receptive to our Triune God.

The third biblical account that surfaces in my thinking is 1 Kings 19:9-13. This short paragraph is a part of the larger story of idolatry and Baal worship in the life of Israel. The bold prophet, Elijah, had confronted King Ahab and then had won a world-class contest over the false prophets of Baal at Mt. Carmel. Yet when the victorious Elijah's life was threatened by Queen Jezebel, he fled in fear as fast as his prophetic legs could carry him. He was alone, undernourished, physically exhausted and hiding in a Mt. Horeb cave when God miraculously provided sleep, bread, water and strength.

I don't know of anyone who described Elijah's entire experience better than Eugene Peterson. Peterson masterfully unfolded the Elijah dullness of God's presence this way. He wrote:

> "… Elijah needs more than a safe place. He needs to recover his prophetic soul. Mount Carmel had knocked the prophetic wind out of him… The angel sends him to Moses' country… Having arrived at 'Horeb the mount of God' (1 Kings 19:8), Elijah found

a cave… On his pilgrimage to Horeb, the mountain of God and of Moses, he recovered his prophetic focus… The pilgrimage did its work: the slow trudge through the wilderness, retracing paths that Moses had walked four hundred years earlier; time on the mountain to reflect on the great prophetic proclamation of the Name, Yahweh, the name that would free human language from turning God into a thing, reducing God to an idea or cause or verbal tool… Yahweh spoke to Elijah and Elijah answered Yahweh. On the mountain and in that cave Yahweh and Elijah got reacquainted… The silence is preceded by wind, earthquake, and fire, not unlike the thunder, lightning, fire, smoke and trumpet blasts that Moses met on this same mountain. Elijah almost certainly expected, after such a Moses prelude, to receive a Moses conclusion in which 'God would answer him in thunder' (Exodus 19:19). But instead of thunder, Yahweh met Elijah in a quiet, inarticulate breathing—God's breath, God's life… Elijah has his breath back, his prophetic breath. He is ready."[103]

On the run, Elijah had hurried past God. He failed to see the God who is alive, the God who is personal and ever-present. He completely missed His nearness. How often have I made that very mistake? Elijah's life, with all of its challenges, reminds us to stay alert to God.

The fourth biblical account that comes to mind is Luke 10:38-42 when Jesus' ministry took Him to Bethany, the town of Lazarus and his sisters, Mary and Martha. It seems that Jesus arrived without much notice yet Martha wanted everything to be perfect. In her hurry and worry, she became "distracted with much serving" (Luke 10:40). Martha's desire to bless Jesus with a perfect meal caused her to chide her sister, Mary, to help her. When that didn't work, Martha implored Jesus to prod Mary. But Jesus, with kindness and tenderness, told Martha, "You are anxious and troubled about many things, but one thing is necessary" (Luke 10:41-42). The one thing that would not be taken away from Mary was her attentiveness in the moment

---

103. Eugene Peterson, *The Jesus Way* (Grand Rapids, MI: Eerdmans, 2007), 113-118.

to the teaching of Jesus. He does not condemn Martha's meal preparations but instead, reminds her that her frantic activity is not the necessary thing in His presence. Martha's failure is not in her service, but in her blindness and deafness to the living reality of God in the person of Christ. This is often my failure too, and perhaps yours.

The last two Scriptural accounts as examples, John 7:1-5 and John 14:1-9, can be combined here. Like the early apprentices of Jesus, I can be miserably unaware of the true Presence. Jesus' brothers did this in John 7 and Jesus' disciple, Philip, did the same thing in the Jerusalem upper room. I know there are other Bible passages that speak to our lack of spiritual receptivity, but these will suffice.

Listen to the sobering insight of Virginia Stem Owens in her wonderful book, *And the Trees Clap their Hands.* She wrote:

> "To spy out the reality hidden in appearances requires vigilance, perseverance. It takes everything I've got. Forty years ago it came easy. Absolutely nothing got by me then. Even now a name, a color, an aroma will come back to me from those early years with extraordinary vividness… For the child, newborn, is a natural spy. Only his inherent limitations impede him from consuming all the clues of the universe fitted to his perceiving capacities… He is devoted to discovery, resists sleep in order to consume more data… Yet gradually, over time, something goes wrong. The spy slowly begins to forget his mission… He forgets what he's about. He goes to school, grows up. He gets his job, collects his pay, buys a house, waters the lawn. He settles down and settles in… Then one morning he wakes up and only yawns. It must be there somewhere, buried in the brain cells, but at least superficially the memory is erased. The spy goes native."[104]

The highest calling of a Jesus follower is to live fully in God's presence and thereby bring glory to Him. Perhaps this is what Paul intended when he

---

104. Virginia Stem Owens, *And the Trees Clap their Hands* (Eugene, OR: Wipf and Stock Publishers, 2005), 4.

told the Thessalonians, "Pray without ceasing" (1 Thessalonians 5:17). The problem is that we have an enemy who seeks to destroy our awareness of God and blunt that receptivity. So, our soul's house requires a consciousness examination. Leighton Ford was right when he observed that the qualities of attentiveness include being fully present in the moment, looking long enough, looking freshly at what is familiar, being available, becoming aware, waiting with expectancy, being mindful and being wakeful.[105] Three questions can help us be more alert to the One who longs for us to know Him and make Him known.

> What tends to stifle spiritual receptivity in me?
>
> Why would I require a "burning bush" experience in order to believe that God wanted to talk with me, spend time with me and awaken me to His presence?
>
> What would have to be rearranged in my soul's house in order to become more spiritually receptive?

As I a child, I thought I could see the whole world from our central Indiana farmhouse. When my family moved to central Illinois, I continued to believe that the entire planet could be seen from my backyard. I imagined, if I looked hard enough, that I could see what others could not. Some who were raised on the prairie disdain the rolling, flat grasslands. They mock the small creeks and wooded landscape and minimize the farms, ponds, lakes and streams that shape this part of North America. The prairie landscape seems unimpressive next to the Rocky Mountains or the mighty oceans that line the coasts of this country. But I see the details of God's transforming hand in places like nearby Kickapoo Creek. The creeks and prairies preach to me

---

[105]. Leighton Ford, *The Attentive Life: Discerning God's Presence in All things* (Downers Grove, IL: IVP, 2008), 37-39.

of Christian spiritual formation's long view. The Kickapoo, though small, has the fingerprints of the Creator on it. Seemingly insignificant landmarks remind me to look for the far-reaching work of our Triune God, even into eternity, even when others cannot or will not see His handiwork.

CONCLUSION

THE SOUL'S HOUSE AND AN ONGOING PRAYER

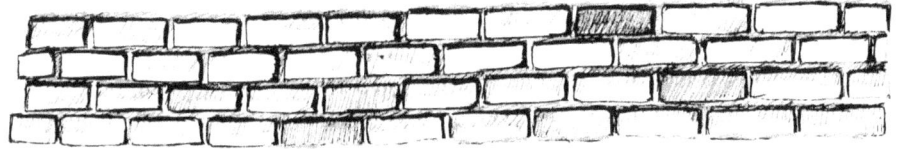

"There is work which God requires to be done by each one of us, and which no one else can do."[106]

My soul's house depends upon our Triune God keeping His promise. The call to a life of discipleship and to the promise of being formed into Jesus' likeness is always on my mind. I believe this promise was ever on Paul's mind too. There is a brief prayer at the close of his first letter to the Thessalonians that I believe is an appropriate conclusion to this primer.

We know from Acts 17 that Paul spent at least three Sabbaths in Thessalonica preaching and teaching in the synagogue. Some Bible students believe that Paul spent nearly three months in Thessalonica proving that Jesus was the Christ and that it was necessary for the Christ to suffer and rise from the dead (Acts 17:2-3). Paul probably wrote this letter from Corinth somewhere around 51 AD. He reminded the Thessalonians of the urgency of Jesus' Second Coming (1 Thessalonians 1:10; 2:19: 3:13; 4:15-17; and 5:23). This underscores the way that our spiritual formation is grounded in

---
106. Underhill, *Concerning the Inner Life*, 133.

the return of our King. Paul ended this first letter with this prayer:

> "Now may the God of peace himself sanctify you completely and may your whole spirit and soul and body be kept blameless at the coming of our Lord Jesus Christ. He who calls you is faithful; he will surely do it" (1 Thessalonians 5:23-24).

Paul had two heartfelt prayer requests for the church in Thessalonica. First, he asked God to sanctify the Thessalonian Jesus followers completely. He prayed that God would make them wholly holy, overlook nothing, and leave nothing in their inner life unaddressed. He asked that no dark closet of iniquity be allowed, and no buried septic tank of sin permitted. Paul prayed for absolute formational perfection. Paul's prayer here reminds me of his prayer for the Philippians when he prayed: "I am sure of this, that he who began a good work in you will bring it to completion at the day of Jesus Christ" (Philippians 1:6).

That prayer is our prayer. We want the part of us that connects with God, our spirit, and our innermost self to be entirely His. We want the house that holds all of this together, the house of the soul, to be devoted completely to Him. We want our physical self, our body, to be an instrument of praise to Him. Nothing short of that will do. That's our prayer and that was Paul's prayer too.

The second part of Paul's prayer was that God would keep the Thessalonians blameless. He literally prayed, "Be blameless at the coming of our Lord Jesus Christ" (I Thessalonians 5:23). He prayed that they would be guarded, protected and preserved free of guilt and free of worry. This prayer points to the ongoing work of the Holy Spirit. This prayer is full of sanctification talk.

This is the very prayer I pray for my own life and for yours. It is the prayer that reminds me that my past, what some might call "positional sanctification," is sealed because of the finished work of Jesus at the cross. This prayer reminds me that my present situation is in my loving King's authoritative control, what some might call "progressive sanctification." This prayer also reminds me that my future formation, what some might call "perfect sanctification," is promised by God to be complete at the return of Jesus. "We know that when He appears, we will be like Him" (1 John 3:2). Our spiritual formation is grounded in the return of Jesus. Why, then, do we grow so impatient with our lack of transformative change, when we feel as if we have made no spiritual progress at all?

While pastoring that small congregation years ago in Lake Fork, Illinois, I planted my first garden. Gardening and gardens were central to that culture, so, I made a garden behind the church building. I planted seeds of sweet corn, green beans, tomatoes, watermelon and assorted spices. I solicited wise advice from the old-timers. I babied that garden. I loved that garden. I watched over that garden, but I grew impatient. I wanted to know if things were growing, so I did the most profoundly stupid thing a gardener can do. I bent down, pulled back the soil of one of the green bean seedlings that I had planted and peeked to see if growth was evident. Sure enough, it was growing! Roots were apparent, but my impatient snooping ended up killing that specific plant. I learned two valuable lessons. First, a seedling's deep roots grow best when left undisturbed. Second, a seedling's maturity is based on the Creator's timeline, not mine. My continual prayer is shaped by Paul's prayer for the Thessalonians.

May our ongoing formation be ever and always for God's glory. May our continual transformation be ever and always for the supremacy of Jesus Christ over everything and everyone. May our past, present and future sanctification be ever and always through the faithful work of the Holy Spirit in the building of our soul's house. May this change be ever and always for our Triune God's eternal purpose. I pray this in the Name of the Father, the Son and the Holy Spirit, Amen.

BIBLIOGRAPHY

Augustine. *The Confessions of St. Augustine.* New York, NY: Doubleday, 1960.

Barth, Karl. *Dogmatics in Outline.* New York, NY: Harper, 1959.

Barrett, Matthew. *None Greater: The Undomesticated Attributes of God.* Grand Rapids, MI: Baker, 2019.

Blomberg, Craig. *Matthew.* Nashville, TN: Broadman Press, 1992.

Boa, Ken. *Conformed to His Image.* Grand Rapids, MI: Zondervan, 2001.

Bonhoeffer, Dietrich. *Life Together.* New York: NY: Harper and Row, 1954.

Bruner, Frederick. *The Christbook:* Matthew 1-12. Revised and Expanded Edition. Grand Rapids, MI: Eerdmans, 2004.

Calhoun, Adele Ahlberg. *Spiritual Disciplines Handbook.* Revised Edition. Downers Grove, IL: IVP, 2015.

Carson, D.A. *Basics for Believers: An Exposition of Philippians.* Grand Rapids, MI: Baker Academic, 1996.

Craddock, Fred. *Philippians: Interpretation A Bible Commentary for Teaching and Preaching.* Atlanta, GA: John Knox Press, 1985.

DeYoung, Kevin. *Crazy Busy.* Wheaton, IL: Crossway, 2013.

Fadling, Alan. *An Unhurried Life.* Downers Grove, IL: IVP, 2013.

Ford, Leighton. *The Attentive Life: Discerning God's Presence in All Things.* Downers Grove, IL: IVP, 2008.

Foster, Richard. *Celebration of Discipline: The Path of Spiritual Growth.* 25th Anniversary. New York, NY: Harper-Collins, 1998.

Goggin, Jamin and Kyle Strobel. *Reading the Christian Spiritual Classics.* Downers Grove, IL: IVP, 2013.

Harris, R.L., G.L. Archer and B.K. Waltke (Editors). *Theological Workbook of the Old Testament: Volume II.* Chicago, IL: Moody Press, 1980.

Hudson, Trever. *Christ-Following: Ten Signposts to Spirituality.* Grand Rapids, MI: Fleming H. Revell, 1996.

Iglesias, Amanda. "For Those With Eyes to See, There is Theological Truth in Church Architecture." *www.christianitytoday.com,* December 8, 2021. https://www.christianitytoday.com/ct/2021/december-web-only/church-architecture-theology-read-elevation-plan-section.html.

Jackman, David. *The Bible Speaks Today: The Message of John's Letters.* Downers Grove, IL: IVP, 1988.

Jacobs, Alan. *Breaking Bread With The Dead: A Reader's Guide to a More Tranquil Mind.* New York, NY: Penguin Press, 2020.

Jones, J.K. *Reading With God in Mind.* Joplin, MO: College Press, 2003.

Jones, J.K. *Waiting on God: Trusting Him in Times of Suffering.* Joplin, MO: College Press, 1996.

Keller, Tim. *Prayer: Experiencing Awe and Intimacy with God.* New York, NY: Penguin Books, 2014.

Koessler, John. *The Radical Pursuit of Rest.* Downers Grove, IL: IVP, 2016.

Lawrence, Brother. *The Practice of the Presence of God with Spiritual Maxims.* Grand Rapids, MI: Fleming H. Revell, 1993.

Lewis, C.S. *The Lion, The Witch, and the Wardrobe.* New York, NY: Harper-Collins, 1994.

Lewis, C.S. *Mere Christianity.* New York, NY: MacMillan, 1956.

Manning, Brennan. *Ruthless Trust.* San Francisco, CA: Harper-Collins, 2000.

Martyr, Justin. *Justin Martyr: The Dialogue with Trypho. Translated by* A. Lukyn Williams. New York, NY: MacMillan Company, 1930.

McKenna, David. *How to Read a Christian Book.* Grand Rapids, MI: Baker Books, 2001.

Metaxas, Eric. *Bonhoeffer: Pastor, Martyr, Prophet, Spy.* New York, NY: Thomas Nelson, 2010.

Morris, Leon. *The Gospel According to Matthew.* Grand Rapids, MI: Eerdmans, 1992.

Moulton, Harold K. *The Challenge of the Concordance.* London, GB: Hollen Street Press, 1977.

Munger, Robert Boyd. *My Heart Christ's Home.* Downers Grove, IL: IVP, 1975.

Ortlund, Dane. *Gentle and Lowly: The Heart of Christ for Sinners and Sufferers.* Wheaton, IL: Crossway, 2020.

Owens, Virginia Stem. *And The Trees Clap Their Hands.* Eugene, OR: Wipf and Stock, 2005.

Packer, J.I. *Knowing God.* Downers Grove, IL: IVP, 1973.

Packer, J.I. *Knowing Scripture.* Downers Grove, IL: IVP, 1979.

Peterson, Eugene H. *As Kingfishers Catch Fire.* Colorado Springs, CO: WaterBrook Books, 2017.

Peterson, Eugene H. *Eat This Book.* Grand Rapids, MI: Eerdmans, 2006.

Peterson, Eugene H. *Take and Read. Spiritual Reading: An Annotated List.* Grand Rapids, MI: Eerdmans, 1996.

Peterson, Eugene H. *The Jesus Way.* Grand Rapids, MI: Eerdmans, 2007.

Platt, David. *Christ-Centered Exposition: Exalting Jesus in Matthew.* Nashville, TN: B&H Publishing, 2013.

Prior, Karen Swallow. *On Reading Well: Finding the Good Life through Great Books.* Grand Rapids, MI: Brazos Press, 2018.

Schaeffer, Francis. *The God Who Is There.* Downers Grove, IL: IVP, 1968.

Sleeth, Matthew. *24/6: A Prescription for a Healthier, Happier Life.* Carol Stream, IL: Tyndale, 2012.

Spurgeon, C.H. *Spurgeon's Lectures to His Students.* Condensed and Abridged by David Otis Fuller. Grand Rapids, MI: Zondervan, 1945.

Stanford, Miles. *The Green Letters: Principles of Spiritual Growth.* Grand Rapids, MI: Zondervan, 1975.

Stott, John R.W. *The Message of 2 Timothy: Guard the Gospel. The Bible Speaks Today.* Downers Grove, IL: IVP, 1973.

Tozer, A.W. *The Knowledge of the Holy.* San Francisco, CA: Harper & Row, 1978.

Tozer, A.W. *The Pursuit of God.* Camp Hill, PA: Christian Publications, 1982.

Um, Stephen. *1 Corinthians: The Word of the Cross.* Wheaton, IL: Crossway, 2015.

Underhill, Evelyn. *Concerning the Inner Life with The House of the Soul.* Eugene, OR: Wipf and Stock, 2004.

Underhill, Evelyn. *The Spiritual Life.* Harrisburg, PA: Morehouse Publishing, 1994.

Villodas, Rich. *The Deeply Formed Life.* Colorado Springs, CO: WaterBrook Books, 2020.

Warren, Tish Harrison. *Liturgy of the Ordinary.* Downers Grove, IL: IVP, 2016.

Whitney, Donald. *Spiritual Disciplines for the Christian Life.* Colorado Springs, CO: NavPress, 1991.

Willett, Don. *Stages of Faith: 8 Milestones that Mark Your Journey.* La Mirada, CA: Biola University, 2005.

Worcester, J.H. *The Life of David Livingstone.* Chicago, IL: Moody Publishers, 1981.

Yancey, Philip. *Where the Light Fell: A Memoir.* Colorado Springs, CO: Convergent Books, 2021.

Young, Jun and David Kinnaman. *The Hyperlinked Life: Live with Wisdom in an Age of Information Overload.* Frames—Barna Group. Grand Rapids, MI: Zondervan, 2013.

ACKNOWLEDGEMENTS

No book is ever completed without the help of others. The influence of Evelyn Underhill's writings has been instrumental in my life, especially *The House of the Soul*. I have accepted from her those words and ideas that match what I believe Scripture teaches, while graciously rejecting those that I believe do not. My friends at College Press have been encouraging, helpful and kind throughout the entire process; I am so very thankful for their partnership. Their technical support is appreciated. Dr. Kent and Sue Taulbee, trusted friends, have helped to make this book a better resource with their encouragements and corrections. Sandi Knapp, faithful co-laborer, spent hours transcribing my lectures into something that became readable and understandable. Jeff Crosby, Evangelical Christian Publishers Association president and CEO, is that rare friend with whom I entrust poorly written first-drafts. I am ever grateful that he is willing to read anything I write. The ongoing support of my beloved wife, children, grandchildren and son-in-law mean more to me than I can put into words. I thank you all for your constant love. As is always true, any mistakes found in this book are entirely mine.

www.ingramcontent.com/pod-product-compliance
Lightning Source LLC
LaVergne TN
LVHW051522070426
835507LV00023B/3248